Copts in Michigan

DISCOVERING THE PEOPLES OF MICHIGAN

Arthur W. Helweg, Russell M. Magnaghi, and Linwood H. Cousins, Series Editors

Ethnicity in Michigan: Issues and People
Jack Glazier and Arthur W. Helweg

Discovering the Peoples of Michigan is a series of publications examining the state's rich multicultural heritage. The series makes available an interesting, affordable, and varied collection of books that enables students and lay readers to explore Michigan's ethnic dynamics. A knowledge of the state's rapidly changing multicultural history has far-reaching implications for human relations, education, public policy, and planning. We believe that Discovering the Peoples of Michigan will enhance understanding of the unique contributions that diverse and often unrecognized communities have made to Michigan's history and culture.

Copts in Michigan

Eliot Dickinson

Michigan State University Press

East Lansing

♾ The paper used in this publication meets the minimum requirements
of ANSI/NISO Z39.48-1992 (R 1997) (Permanence of Paper).

Michigan State University Press
East Lansing, Michigan 48823-5245

Printed and bound in the United States of America.

14 13 12 11 10 09 08   1 2 3 4 5 6 7 8 9 10

ISBN: 978-0-87013-824-9

LIBRARY OF CONGRESS CATALOGING-IN-PUBLICATION DATA
Dickinson, Eliot.
Copts in Michigan / Eliot Dickinson.
p. cm. — (Discovering the peoples of Michigan)
Includes bibliographical references and index.
ISBN 978-0-87013-824-9 (pbk. : alk. paper)
1. Egyptian Americans—Michigan—History. 2. Copts—Michigan—History. 3. Immigrants—Michigan—
History. 4. Social networks—Michigan—History. 5. Michigan—Ethnic relations. 6. Michigan—Social life
and customs. 7. Michigan—Religious life and customs. 8. Detroit (Mich.)—Ethnic relations. 9. Detroit
(Mich.)—Social life and customs. 10. Detroit (Mich.)—Religious life and customs. I. Title.
F575.E38D53 2008
977.40088'28172—dc22
2008015192

Discovering the Peoples of Michigan. The editors wish to thank
the Kellogg Foundation for their generous support.

Cover design by Ariana Grabec-Dingman
Book design by Sharp Des!gns, Lansing, Michigan
Cover photo: Building community spirit at the St. Mina Retreat Center
in Mio, Michigan (courtesy of Soli Soliman)

Michigan State University Press is a member of the Green Press Initiative and is committed to de-
veloping and encouraging ecologically responsible publishing practices. For more information
about the Green Press Initiative and the use of recycled paper in book publishing, please visit *www.
greenpressinitiative.org.*

Visit Michigan State University Press on the World Wide Web at *www.msupress.msu.edu*

To my Mother,
and in memory of Victor Manious

ACKNOWLEDGMENTS

I would like to thank the many people who helped me complete this work. I am grateful to my friend and bibliophile extraordinaire, John W. Smith, and his wife for generously putting me up in their home while I conducted field research in the Detroit area. Special thanks are due to Dr. Ronald R. Stockton at the University of Michigan–Dearborn for his insightful comments and for sharing his findings from the "Detroit Arab American Study," and to Dr. Claude F. Jacobs, Director of the Pluralism Project at the University of Michigan–Dearborn. Jonathan Roach and the staff at the Ecumenical Theological Seminary Library in Detroit were consummately professional, helpful, and friendly. My respect and admiration goes to Fathers Mina Essak and Maximus Habib, as well as the many members of the Coptic community in Michigan who so charitably shared their time and opened their hearts and homes to me: Victor, Soheir, and Yustina Manious; Botros Soliman; Dr. Roushdy Boulos; Dr. Anis Milad; Dr. Adel Abadeer; Dr. Soli Soliman; Joanne Aneese; and Fady Ibrahim. I greatly appreciate the efforts of Peter Stehouwer, who skillfully procured for me copies of the obsolete *Peace News* from the Library of Congress. Many thanks also to Rachel Bishop at the Hope College Library, to my research assistant, Alisha Philo, and to my colleagues Dr. John Quinn and Dr. Boyd Wilson for their careful proofreading and valuable feedback.

SERIES ACKNOWLEDGMENTS

Discovering the Peoples of Michigan is a series of publications that resulted from the cooperation and effort of many individuals. The people recognized here are not a complete representation, for the list of contributors is too numerous to mention. However, credit must be given to Jeffrey Bonevich, who worked tirelessly with me on contacting people as well as researching and organizing material.

The initial idea for this project came from Mary Erwin, but I must thank Fred Bohm, director of the Michigan State University Press, for seeing the need for this project, for giving it his strong support, and for making publication possible. Also, the tireless efforts of Keith Widder and Elizabeth Demers, senior editors at Michigan State University Press, were vital in bringing DPOM to fruition.

Otto Feinstein and Germaine Strobel of the Michigan Ethnic Heritage Studies Center patiently and willingly provided names for contributors and constantly gave this project their tireless support. Yvonne Lockwood of the Michigan State University Museum has also suggested and advised contributors.

Many of the maps in the series were prepared by Gregory Anderson at the Geographical Information Center (GIS) at Western Michigan University under the directorship of David Dickason. Additional maps have been contributed by Ellen White.

Other authors and organizations provided comments on other aspects of the work. There are many people that were interviewed by the various authors who will remain anonymous. However, they have enabled the story of their group to be told. Unfortunately, their names are not available, but we are grateful for their cooperation.

Most of all, this work is a tribute to the writers who patiently gave their time to write and share their research findings. Their contributions are noted and appreciated. To them goes most of the gratitude.

ARTHUR W. HELWEG, *Series Co-editor*

Contents

Introduction

A drive from the concrete jungle of downtown Detroit, through the harrowing rush of oncoming traffic and the sound and fury of the sprawling metropolis, to the affluent northern suburb of Troy, where St. Mark Coptic Orthodox Church is located, presents a study in marked contrasts. For sitting with Father Mina Essak in his beautiful quiet church, amongst long rows of wooden pews and Coptic icons of St. Mark and St. Mary, and discussing the story of the Copts, or Egyptian Christians, in Michigan is as soothing as it is edifying. Father Mina,[1] as he is affectionately known, is a gentle man with brown eyes, a long grey beard, a keen intellect, and an endearing Egyptian accent. He is the quintessential embodiment of a Coptic priest, who cares for his flock and his church with great devotion, and, exemplifying the Coptic community as a whole, is one of the most generous people anyone is likely to meet.

The Copts in Michigan are a relatively small and tight-knit ethno-religious group, numbering perhaps three thousand people and living mostly in the Detroit area. They are comparative newcomers to the state, arriving mostly since the mid-1960s, and as a group they tend to be highly educated, with a professional predilection for engineering and medicine. They have much to be thankful for, as their numbers have grown over the years and their church, which relies strictly on donations from the congregation, has expanded at an impressive rate. Their ancestral home is Egypt, the ancient cradle of human civilization and, according to biblical narrative, erstwhile sanctuary of Jesus Christ.

However, Copts are leaving Egypt due to relative economic deprivation and severe religious persecution, which is fueled by historical enmity between Muslims and Christians and exacerbated by the wars in Iraq and Afghanistan. While such human rights abuses as are occurring in contemporary Egypt should be an outrage to the global community, the deteriorating situation continues unabated, leaving the Copts to their dark night of the soul. In Michigan, by contrast, they are flourishing, living their American dream, building their version of a shining city on a hill, and playing a significant role in what is otherwise a global Coptic renaissance. This is their story.[2]

Who Are the Copts?

One oft-cited theory is that the word "Copt" is derived from the name of the ancient Egyptian capital city of Hikaptah, which literally meant "house of the spirit of Ptah" in the language of the pharaohs.[3] It is thought that the Greeks phonetically corrupted the city's name into *Aigyptios,* their word for the inhabitants of Egypt.[4] Thereafter, the Arabs added to this phonetic change in the seventh century A.D. by calling Egypt *dar al-Qubt* (or *dar al-Qibt*), Arabic for "home of the Egyptians." The Arabic *Qubt* was then further modified in the European languages as *Copte* in French, *Kopte* in German, and Copt in English. This etymological examination thus reveals how the "kapt" in Hikaptah likely evolved—or perhaps devolved—successively into *Aigyptios, Qubt,* and Copt. In this original sense, the word "Copt" is synonymous with "Egyptian."

The renowned coptologist Pierre du Bourguet correctly notes that "defining the word 'Copt' is not an easy matter. Gratuitous applications of the term in many circumstances have come together under the Coptic umbrella, resulting in a surprising mixture of connotations. A definition, therefore, that considers factual usage or acceptable conventional usage becomes necessary."[5] It follows, then, that a basic set of definitions is necessary in order to proceed, for determining who the Copts are is a sine qua non of any learned conception, and fruitful analysis, of the Coptic community.

It is perhaps fitting to first examine how the Copts, or more specifically the spokesmen of the Coptic Orthodox Church—the oldest representative institution of the Coptic community—see and define themselves. In *The Coptic Orthodox Church: A Lily Among Thorns,* Dr. Raafat Fahim Gindi explains: "Coptic: It means Egyptian, the word Copt is derived from 'Gypt' in Aegyptius which is the Greek name of Egypt. It is now restricted to the Christians of Egypt to distinguish them from the Moslems. Also, it applies to those who believe in the Coptic Orthodox Church."[6] Other regularly accepted definitions are similar: a Copt is commonly understood to be "one of the natives of Egypt descended from the Ancient Egyptians," or "a member of the Coptic Church," and Coptic is "the extinct language of Egypt that developed from ancient Egyptian, now used liturgically by the Coptic Church."[7]

Thus, the Copts are an ethnic group that, as Max Weber famously put it, entertains "a subjective belief in their common descent because of similarities of physical type or of customs or both, or because of memories of colonization and migration."[8] They are also a religious group defined by membership in the Coptic Orthodox Church, so that, in theory, anyone can become a Copt through conversion to Coptic Orthodox Christianity. While these are the basic definitions that set the parameters for the following exploration of the Coptic community in Michigan, there are a number of inescapably vexatious, but nevertheless germane, questions that arise when discussing the Copts.

Just as Friedrich Nietzsche once said that "it is characteristic of the Germans that the question: 'What is German?' never dies out among them,"[9] there are also people who quibble about what it means to be a Copt and who can be one. The Coptic Orthodox Church is in communion with the Armenian, Indian, Syrian, Eritrean, and Ethiopian churches (known collectively as the Oriental Orthodox Churches), and it is the mother church of the latter two. To what extent can members of the Ethiopian Orthodox Tewahedo Church and Eritrean Orthodox Tewahedo Church, of which there are perhaps as many as forty million, be considered Coptic? And what about the Coptic Catholic Church, which is in communion with the Roman Catholic Church but headed by Archbishop Antonios Naguib, the Coptic Catholic patriarch of Alexandria? Are Copts who have joined Protestant churches, or converted to Islam, still Coptic? Lastly, can Muslim Egyptians who identify as descendents of the ancient pharaohs justifiably claim to be Copts?

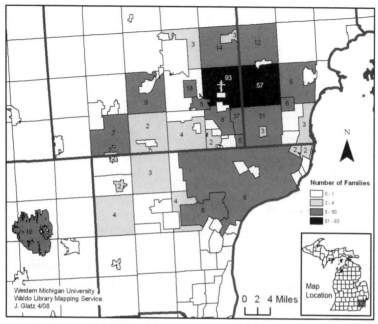

Distribution of the members of St. Mark's Coptic Orthodox Church. Sources: Michigan Center for Geographic Information, Author.

Further complicating the matter of definitions is the existence of religious and spiritual groups in the United States who claim to be Coptic. There is, for example, the True Temple of Solomon Church in Highland Park in Detroit, which says it is a branch of the Coptic Church. Its Web site has a picture of the sun setting over the pyramids at Giza, as well as camels in the desert, and asserts that the Bible is a "Black History Book" and that "Jesus was a Black Man!!!"[10] And then there is the Coptic Fellowship International, which is based in Wyoming, Michigan, and held its annual conference in Olivet, Michigan, in June 2007. The Fellowship espouses a philosophy centered on the mysteries of ancient Egypt and is comprised of new-age American spiritualists seeking positive personal and planetary change through right thinking, good energy, and projecting light and love.[11]

The important point is that there are numerous conceivable definitions of the words "Copt" and "Coptic," ranging from the legitimate to the spurious.

Some people self-identify as Copts even though they are neither of Egyptian descent nor members of the Coptic Orthodox Church. Others remain rigid in their ideas about who can be a Copt, as exemplified in the true story of Father Mark, an American who converted from Catholicism, spent an extended amount of time in Egypt, and became a priest in the Coptic Orthodox Church. A skeptical Egyptian national asked him, "What kind of a priest are you anyway?" to which he replied, "I am a Coptic Orthodox Priest." The Egyptian inquisitor then countered, "You may, for all I know, be an Orthodox priest, but a Copt you will never be. You have to be born a Copt to be a Copt. I was born in Egypt. I am a Copt."[12] While this anecdote reveals an exclusionary sense of belonging, it also shows how a non-Egyptian can become a Copt—in the religious rather than the ethnic sense.

In terms of how the above examples relate to the definitions I have set forth, I believe that Father Mark can be considered Coptic, whereas members of the True Temple of Solomon Church and the Coptic Fellowship International cannot. Of the aforementioned Oriental Orthodox Churches, which are in communion with the Coptic Orthodox Church, the Ethiopian and Eritrean are most closely related to the Copts in a tangential liturgical sense. I concur with Pierre du Bourguet's assertion that "the word 'Copt' is to be discarded when discussing the Syro-Jacobites and the Armenians and whatever may concern them. Nor can it designate the Ethiopians, who are of a different race and language. But it may be used to describe ecclesiastical and administrative affairs such as their dogma and liturgy. Concerning Ethiopians, it is normal to speak of the Coptic hierarchy, Coptic Christians, and Coptic liturgy."[13] Coptic Catholics and converts fall into a gray area, and their exact nomenclature is open to debate.[14] Lastly, Egyptian Muslims may legitimately claim to be the descendents of the ancient Egyptians, but they do not self-identify as Coptic, in large part because Coptic has become synonymous with Christian.[15]

I recognize that determining who belongs, or does not, to any particular ethno-religious group is a subjective endeavor. My intention is not to inflame sensitivities, or split hairs, but rather to provide a clear social-scientific analysis of the issue at hand. That said, the Copts described in this study are primarily Egyptian Christian immigrants and their families, and members of the Coptic Orthodox Church. This baseline understanding provides a conceptual foundation from which to proceed, facilitating a first step toward determining the size, makeup, and characteristics of the Coptic community in Michigan.

How Many Copts Are There?

It is difficult to determine the size of the Coptic population with any certainty, whether in Egypt, the United States, or Michigan. In Egypt the issue is contentious and long-standing, with political implications for both the majority Muslims and minority Christians. The Copts, seeing strength in numbers and wanting the world to know what they believe is their true size, tend to inflate their numbers, while the Muslim-dominated government, in turn, habitually under-represents the size and number of the Coptic population. The official and unofficial figures vary widely and should, therefore, be taken *cum grano salis*—that is, with a grain of salt and a measured degree of skepticism.

Throughout most of the twentieth century, decennial census data reported that the Copts made up between 6 and 8 percent of the Egyptian population. The official 1976 Egyptian census registered 2,315,560 Copts, or 6.31 percent of the total population, a figure that the Copts decried as offensive and deliberately erroneous.[16] Subsequent reports found that 6 percent of a population of 50,525,000 was "Coptic or other" in 1986, and in 1996 the count was again 6 percent out of a total population of 63,575,107.[17] By 2006 the number of Copts jumped to an estimated 9 percent of a total population of 78,887,007 Egyptians.[18] Precisely what explains this jump is unclear, but it is more likely a reflection of an adjusted estimate rather than a sudden Coptic baby boom. Perhaps the most striking aspect of these numbers is the marked increase in the size of the total population, indicating that modern Egypt is growing at an impressively rapid pace.

While these are the official numbers, the Copts and their advocates argue that their real size is closer to ten million, or well over 10 percent of the population. Some estimates run much higher, and often the Copts are given the benefit of the doubt by sympathetic scholars. The 1980 *Harvard Encyclopedia of American Ethnic Groups,* for example, states liberally that the Copts "form less than a fourth of the population of Egypt."[19] At the end of the day, however, it is probably safe to say that the true number lies somewhere between the government's low census count and the higher figure promoted by members of the Coptic Orthodox Church.

Determining the size of the Coptic community in the United States is, mercifully, void of the political drama found in Egypt, but nonetheless cannot be done with accuracy. This is because Coptic immigrants are classified generally as Egyptians rather than specifically as Egyptian Christians. According to the 1970 American census, there were 31,358 Egyptian immigrants in the United States, of which an estimated 25,000 were Copts.[20] In the late 1970s, Coptic leaders estimated that there were between 85,000 and 100,000 Copts in the United States, and by 1989 estimates ranged between 160,000 and 180,000.[21] According to data from the 2000 United States census and the National Council of Churches, there are approximately one hundred Coptic Orthodox Churches in the United States, with an estimated total of 300,000 members.[22] The largest communities are found in America's major metropolitan areas, such as New York, Jersey City, Boston, Los Angeles, Chicago, Detroit, Houston, and Cleveland.

The number of Copts living in Michigan is again an estimate. In *Ethnic Groups in Michigan* the late Mansour Sidhom wrote the following: "The Coptic Community in Michigan is not as stable as communities in other areas of the U.S. because (1) Michigan's warm weather season is not long enough and (2) there is a lack of jobs here making living elsewhere look more promising. For example, 12,000 Copts reside in Los Angeles, California (a large percentage of these people were originally from Michigan); however, there are only about 500 families or approximately 3,000 Copts in the state of Michigan at the present time [1983]—with the majority residing in the Detroit area."[23] Precisely how Sidhom defined a Copt and arrived at this calculation of five hundred families and a total population of three thousand is unknown.

According to the U.S. census, in 2000 there were 115,284 Arabs in the state of Michigan, of whom 3,310 were of Egyptian descent.[24] As there is no government census count of the Copts in Michigan, a tally of the membership of the one Coptic church—that is, the only one recognized by the Coptic Orthodox Church of Alexandria—in the state provides the best possible estimate. According to Father Mina Essak of St. Mark Orthodox Church in Troy, Michigan, as of 2007 around 520 families belong to the church (see Appendix 1 for an interview with Father Mina). If each family consisted of two parents and between two and four children, then there would be between 2,080 and 3,120 Copts affiliated with the church. Obviously, not all Copts in Michigan are members of St. Mark Church, so the statewide total is surely higher.

A content analysis of St. Mark Church's 2006 membership directory confirms that the vast majority of Copts still live in the Detroit metropolitan area, with the largest concentration of families residing in the northern suburbs of Troy, Sterling Heights, Madison Heights, and Warren. It should be noted that Troy, Madison Heights, Bloomfield Hills, and Rochester Hills are in Oakland County, the wealthiest county in Michigan and one of the wealthiest in the entire United States. Ann Arbor, Lansing, and Grand Rapids also have communities large enough to celebrate the liturgy, and are visited once a month by either Father Maximus Habib or Father Mina Essak, the two priests of St. Mark Coptic Church. This breakdown provides a rough sketch of the number and location of the Coptic families in Michigan, as measured by the membership of St. Mark Coptic Orthodox Church in Troy. Admittedly, this is a sketch rather than a complete picture, as nonobservant Copts are omitted, but it nevertheless represents the most solid data available.

Historical Legacy

A ncient Egypt holds a special place in the modern imagination, which is in-
formed by schoolroom history lessons, films, and visits to museums filled
with Egyptian artifacts. One is reminded, perhaps, of the ancient Egyptian
dynasties in the Nile River Valley, of mummies, hieroglyphs, the sphinx, and
the pharaohs—or perhaps of the great pyramids at Giza, long considered a
wonder of the world. As the historian James Henry Breasted put it nearly a
century ago, "the roots of modern civilization are planted deeply in the highly
elaborate life of those nations which rose into power over six thousand years
ago, in the basin of the eastern Mediterranean, and the adjacent regions on
the east of it."[25] This history is part of the splendid inheritance of the Copts in
Michigan, many of whom see themselves as the original Egyptians and di-
rect descendents of the ancient pharaohs. It is what helps shape the identity
of the Copts, creating a sense of community and of placement in time and
space. The historical record reveals how the Coptic script evolved, how the
Copts became and remained Christian, and why Copts in Egypt and Coptic
immigrants in Michigan speak Arabic.

Language, Christianity, and the Church

The Coptic historical narrative, from the ancient past up to the present,
has been heavily influenced by the Greeks, the Arabs, and Christianity. The

Greeks exercised immense influence not only on the Mediterranean, Europe, and the course of Western Civilization, but also on Egypt. The Egyptian city of Alexandria, once renowned for its library and scholarship, still bears the name of Alexander the Great, who conquered Egypt in 332 B.C., and made Greek the official language of Egypt. One of the most significant and lasting consequences of the Greek presence in Egypt was the transcription of Egyptian hieroglyphics using the Greek alphabet, which became the written form of the Coptic language.

Hieroglyphic was the pictographic script, or pictorial writing, used by the ancient Egyptians. The word "hieroglyph" is derived from the Greek and literally means sacred (hiero) writing (glyph). It was beautifully drawn and colored, but with around four thousand symbols comprised an extremely complex writing system. As a result, hieroglyphic was successively simplified into hieratic (meaning priestly) and then demotic (derived from the Greek "demos," meaning people), a more popular script used mostly for secular purposes. Demotic was then transliterated using the Greek alphabet, which, with the addition of seven demotic letters, became Coptic. The Coptic script emerged after the Greek conquest of Egypt, became more common after the first century A.D., and experienced its golden age in the fourth and fifth centuries A.D., a time when Christianity also blossomed in Egypt.

Christianity has a strong and marked connection to Egypt, of which the Copts are rightly proud. Biblical references to Egypt abound—there are over six hundred—including the oft-cited verses "In that day shall there be an altar to the Lord in the midst of the land of Egypt," and "Out of Egypt I have called my Son."[26] According to the Bible, the Holy Family of Joseph, Mary, and Jesus fled to Egypt to escape Herod's decree to kill all of the baby boys in Bethlehem. To this day, visitors to Egypt can trace the route presumably taken by Baby Jesus and his parents. Father Mina Essak of St. Mark Coptic Orthodox Church in Troy says of Jesus' time in Egypt, "it is the only country outside Palestine that the Lord visited while he was on earth. . . . He was there about two years. He drank from the River Nile. He talked the Egyptian language of that time. . . . We of Egypt are very proud of it. We call Egypt a holy land where the Lord has dwelt in our midst."[27]

In approximately A.D. 41 (the exact date is subject to speculation), St. Mark the Evangelist, author of the oldest of the four canonical Gospels, is believed to have arrived in Alexandria, Egypt.[28] As a result of St. Mark's

St. Mark the Evangelist

St. Mark the Evangelist is credited with bringing Christianity to Egypt in the first century A.D. and is seen as the first patriarch of the Coptic Orthodox Church. The earliest and shortest of the four Gospels of the New Testament, the Gospel According to Mark, bears his name. Biblical lore paints an intriguing picture of him, as he is presumed to be one of seventy-two disciples appointed by Jesus (Luke 10:1), and it is thought that he was the man carrying water to the Last Supper (Mark 14:13), as well as running away naked at Jesus's arrest at Gethsemane (Mark 14:51–52).

Coptic icon of St. Mark the Evangelist. Courtesy of Eliot Dickinson.

According to tradition, St. Mark accompanied St. Barnabas and St. Paul on their mission to Antioch (Acts 12:25), and went later with St. Paul to Cyprus (Acts 15:36–40). He is perhaps best known for his journey to Alexandria, Egypt, where he founded the Coptic Church. But for his efforts there he was bitterly resented—Christianity threatened both the ancient Egyptian and Greco-Roman beliefs—and killed on April 25, A.D. 67. His burial place has long been disputed. Italian pirates claim to have taken his remains to Venice, while Copts in Egypt maintain that his head was kept in St. Mark Coptic Orthodox Church in Alexandria.

Many Coptic Orthodox Churches in the United States are named after St. Mark, including the one in Troy, Michigan, which was consecrated in 1981 by Bishop Antonious Markos. The icon of St. Mark is ubiquitous in Coptic churches and usually consists of St. Mark spreading the Gospel in Egypt, with the Mediterranean Sea and the Lighthouse of Alexandria in the background, a lion at his feet, and a fruit tree to symbolize that his work in Africa has borne fruit.

evangelizing, he is credited with bringing Christianity to Egypt and is seen as the first patriarch and founder of the Coptic Orthodox Church. He is not only a preeminent historical figure, but also a ubiquitous eponymous hero among the Copts. Today, St. Mark often comes to mind when a child (e.g., Mark), priest (Father Mark), or church (St. Mark) is to be given a name. In order to facilitate the spread of Christianity, the scriptures were translated in the third and fourth centuries A.D. into Coptic for the benefit of the masses. Thus, Coptic writing flourished concurrently with Christianity. Most profoundly, the Bible was translated into four different dialects of Coptic (Bohairic, Fayumic, Sahidic, and Akhmimic), and while only fragments of these exist today, they remain a source of great pride among the Copts. Part of the emotional power and symbolic significance of the Coptic script comes from the notion that it represents the way Christianity was spread in Egypt nearly two thousand years ago. It is a beautiful reminder that Coptic Christians are members of one of the earliest branches of Christianity.

The Coptic Orthodox Church of Alexandria was known simply as the Egyptian Church until the nineteenth century, when it became known as Coptic Orthodox in order to distinguish its Coptic members from members of other churches, such as the Greek Orthodox Church and the Roman Catholic Church. It is now commonly referred to simply as the Coptic Church. Since St. Mark the Evangelist's arrival in Egypt in the first century A.D., the Coptic Church has been led by an unbroken succession of 117 patriarchs leading up to the current Pope Shenouda III.

The Coptic Church is in communion with the Oriental Orthodox Churches, which are known as non-Chalcedonian. For all but a minority of clerics and scholars, the subtle theological distinctions between the non-Chalcedonian Oriental Orthodox Churches and the Chalcedonian Eastern Orthodox and Roman Catholic Churches are nothing more than esoteric abstractions. In brief, however, it suffices to say that the former split from the latter after the Council of Chalcedon in A.D. 451, where it was decided that Jesus Christ was one person in two fully united natures, one divine and one human (referred to as dyophysite). The churches that rejected this understanding of Christ's nature and stayed true to the three Ecumenical Councils of Nicea, Constantinople, and Ephesus, were henceforth called non-Chalcedonian. They maintained that the union of the human and divine in Christ comprised but one nature (referred to as monophysite or miaphysite).[29]

Pope Shenouda III

Pope Shenouda III is the 117th patriarch of the Coptic Church. He was born Nazir Gayed on August 3, 1923, in Asyut in Upper Egypt, and was raised by his older brother after the deaths of his mother in his infancy and father in his youth. He earned a B.A. in history from Cairo University in 1947, was an infantry officer in the Palestinian war in 1948, and earned a degree from the Coptic Theological Seminary in Cairo in 1949. On July 18, 1954, he joined the al-Suryan Monastery in Western Egypt, living ascetically (for some years allegedly in a cave) as a monk and taking the name Father Antonious al-Suryani. After being ordained as a bishop by Pope Cyril VI, he took the name Shenouda (after St. Shenouda the Archimandrite [A.D. 333–451], Pope Shenouda I [A.D. 859–80], and Pope Shenouda II [A.D. 1032–46]).

After the death of Pope Cyril VI, a congress of seven hundred electors, including forty from the Ethiopian Orthodox Tewahedo Church, nominated three men for the Coptic papacy: Bishop Samuel, Bishop Shenouda, and Father Timotheos. A blindfolded boy from the congregation randomly selected Shenouda in a lottery drawing on October 31, 1971. Since then Pope Shenouda has overseen the revival of the Coptic Church, helped in the growth of the Coptic diaspora, and encouraged the teaching and learning of the Coptic language. His papacy has not been without controversy, however, as he was exiled by Egyptian president Anwar Sadat in 1981 and subsequently released by Hosni Mubarak in 1985. He has also taken an Arab nationalist stance against the state of Israel and threatened to excommunicate Copts who visit there.

Pope Shenouda III visited Michigan in 1977 to lay the cornerstone of St. Mark Church, in 1989, in 1994, in 2003, and again in August 2007 to receive an honorary doctorate of humanities from Lawrence Technological University. He is much loved by the Copts in Michigan, just as many Roman Catholics adored the late Pope John Paul II and revere the current Pope Benedict XVI.

To my mind, these Christological disagreements provide an archetypal example of the narcissism of minor differences. Nevertheless, the schisms that emerged between the Oriental Orthodox Churches on the one side, and the Eastern Orthodox and Roman Catholic Churches on the other, persist to the present day.[30] Following the Council of Chalcedon, a power struggle ensued in Alexandria, Egypt, between the non-Chalcedonian Egyptian (Coptic) pope and a competing Chalcedonian Melkite (Greek Orthodox) pope. Worse, Copts were accused of heresy, persecuted, and even slaughtered by the Melkite patriarchs who were appointed under the Byzantine Eastern Roman Empire, in particular by Cyrus, the Byzantine prefect and bishop of Alexandria who ruled from A.D. 631 to 641.

An army of about four thousand Arabs conquered Egypt between A.D. 639 and 641, bringing with them the Arabic language and Islam, both of which spread rapidly. In much of the literature on Coptic Christianity the Arab arrival is derisively referred to as an "invasion."[31] From the seventh century A.D. onward, Egyptians converted to Islam on a large scale, and Arabic was made the official language in the eighth century A.D. Sometime during the ninth century A.D. Christians permanently crossed over from being a majority to a minority of the Egyptian population.[32] Many Egyptians were forced to convert to Islam,[33] and many were compelled to speak Arabic in order to keep their jobs. Because Copts were Christian rather than Muslim, they had to pay a special tax called the *Jizyah*. In addition to this religious persecution by way of economic punishment, the Coptic language was also suppressed. The Arab Caliph al-Hakim bi-Amr Illah (literally "the ruler by order of God"), who ruled from A.D. 996 to 1020, threatened to cut out the tongues of Egyptians who spoke Coptic. Unsurprisingly, both written and spoken Coptic gradually declined and gave way to Arabic, so that by the seventeenth century Coptic was essentially a dead language.

The Coptic language was preserved within the Coptic Orthodox Church and in the Egyptian monasteries, but even these last bastions eventually acquiesced to spoken and written Arabic. In present-day Egypt Coptic is confined mostly to hymns and prayers, while Arabic is the primary language used to conduct the liturgy and write religious texts. In the United States, English and Arabic are the principle languages used in the liturgy, although the communal prayer book, called *The Divine Liturgies of Saints Basil, Gregory, and Cyril,* includes English, Coptic, and Arabic scripts side by side.[34] When reading the "The Lord's Prayer" in these three languages, and with knowledge of Egypt's history as outlined above, one cannot help but wonder to what extent Copts today associate the pervasive Arabization and Islamization of Egypt, whether on a conscious or subconscious level, with religious and linguistic oppression.

THE OFFERING OF EVENING AND MORNING INCENSE	Ⲡⲧⲁⲗⲟ Ⲩⲡⲓⲥⲑⲟⲓⲛⲟⲩϥⲓ ⲛ̄ⲧⲉ Ⲑⲁⲛⲁⲣⲟⲩⲍⲓ ⲛⲉⲙ Ⲑⲁⲛⲁⲧⲟⲩⲓ	رفع بخور عشية وباكر

The priest uncovers his head, stands at the door of the sanctuary, and says:

يكشـــف الكاهـــن رأسه ويقف أمام باب الهيكل
ويقول:

| Priest:
Have mercy on us, O God, the Father, the Pantocrator. All-Holy Trinity, have mercy on us. | Ⲡⲓ̀ⲡⲣⲉⲥⲃ̄ⲩⲧⲉⲣⲟⲥ:
Ⲉⲗⲉⲏ̀ⲥⲟⲛ ⲏ̀ⲙⲁⲥ ⲟ̀ Ⲑⲉⲟⲥ ⲟ̀ Ⲡⲁⲧⲏⲣ ⲟ̀ ⲡⲁⲛⲧⲟⲕⲣⲁⲧⲱⲣ: ⲡⲁⲛⲁ̀ⲅⲓⲁ ⲧ̀ⲣⲓⲁⲥ ⲉ̀ⲗⲉⲏ̀ⲥⲟⲛ ⲏ̀ⲙⲁⲥ. | يقول الكاهن:
إرحَمنا يا الله الآبُ ضابطَ الكـــل. أيها الثالوثُ القدوسُ ارحَمنا. |
| O Lord, God of the powers, be with us, for we have no helper in our tribulations and afflictions but You. | Ⲡ̄ϭ̄ⲟⲓⲥ Ⲫⲛⲟⲩϯ ⲛ̀ⲧⲉ ⲛⲓⲍⲟⲙ ϣⲱⲡⲓ ⲛⲉⲙⲁⲛ: ϫⲉ ⲙ̀ⲙⲟⲛ ⲛ̀ⲧⲁⲛ ⲛⲟⲩⲃⲟⲏⲑⲟⲥ ϧⲉⲛ ⲛⲉⲛⲑ̀ⲗⲓⲯⲓⲥ ⲛⲉⲙ ⲛⲉⲛⲍⲟⲭⲍⲉⲭ ⲉ̀ⲃⲏⲗ ⲉ̀ⲣⲟⲕ. | أيها الربُ إلهُ القواتِ كُن معـــنا لأنه ليس لنا معينٌ في شدائدنا وضيقاتنا سواكَ. |

Then he says the Lord's Prayer.

ثم يقول الصلاة الربانية:

| Our Father who art in heavens, hallowed be Thy name. Thy kingdom come, Thy will be done, on earth as it is in heaven. Give us this day our daily bread; and forgive us our trespasses, as we forgive those who trespass against us; and lead us not into temptation, but deliver us from the evil one. In Christ Jesus our Lord, for Thine is the kingdom and the power and the glory forever. Amen. | Ϫⲉ Ⲡⲉⲛⲓⲱⲧ ⲉⲧϧⲉⲛ ⲛⲓⲫⲏⲟⲩⲓ: ⲙⲁⲣⲉϥⲧⲟⲩⲃⲟ ⲛ̄ϫⲉ ⲡⲉⲕⲣⲁⲛ: ⲙⲁⲣⲉⲥ̀ⲓ ⲛ̄ϫⲉ ⲧⲉⲕⲙⲉⲧⲟⲩⲣⲟ: ⲡⲉⲧⲉⲍ̀ⲛⲁⲕ ⲙⲁⲣⲉϥϣⲱⲡⲓ ⲙ̀ⲫⲣⲏϯ ϧⲉⲛ ⲧ̀ⲫⲉ ⲛⲉⲙ ⲍⲓϫⲉⲛ ⲡⲓⲕⲁⲍⲓ: ⲡⲉⲛⲱⲓⲕ ⲛ̄ⲧⲉ ⲣⲁⲥϯ ⲙⲏⲓϥ ⲛⲁⲛ ⲙ̀ⲫⲟⲟⲩ: ⲟⲩⲟⲍ ⲭⲁ ⲛⲏⲉⲧⲉⲣⲟⲛ ⲛⲁⲛ ⲉ̀ⲃⲟⲗ: ⲙ̀ⲫⲣⲏϯ ⲍⲱⲛ ⲛ̀ⲧⲉⲛⲭⲱ ⲉ̀ⲃⲟⲗ ⲛ̀ⲛⲏⲉ̀ⲧⲉ ⲟⲩⲟⲛ ⲛ̀ⲧⲁⲛ ⲉ̀ⲣⲱⲟⲩ ⲟⲩⲟⲍ ⲙ̀ⲡⲉⲣⲉⲛⲧⲉⲛ ⲉ̀ϧⲟⲩⲛ ⲉ̀ⲡⲓⲣⲁⲥⲙⲟⲥ ⲁⲗⲗⲁ ⲛⲁⲍⲙⲉⲛ ⲉ̀ⲃⲟⲗ ⲍⲁ ⲡⲓⲡⲉⲧⲍⲱⲟⲩ. ϧⲉⲛ Ⲡⲓⲭ̀ⲣⲓⲥⲧⲟⲥ Ⲓⲏⲥⲟⲩⲥ Ⲡⲉⲛϭ̄ⲟⲓⲥ: ϫⲉ ⲑⲱⲕ ⲧⲉ ϯⲙⲉⲧⲟⲩⲣⲟ ⲛⲉⲙ ϯϫⲟⲙ ⲛⲉⲙ ⲡⲓⲱⲟⲩ ϣⲁ ⲉⲛⲉⲍ ⲁ̀ⲙⲏⲛ. | أبانا الذي في السموات، ليتقدس اسْمُك ليأتِ ملكوتُك لـــتكن مشـــيئتُك، كما في السماء كذلك على الأرض، خبزنا الذي للغد أعطنا اليومَ، واغفر لنا ذنوبَنا كما نغفر نحنُ أيضاً للمذنبين إلينا ولا تدخلنا في تجربة لكن نجنا من الشرير. بالمسيح يسوع ربنا، لأن لـــكَ الملكُ والقوةُ والمجدُ إلى الأبدِ. آمين. |

Page one of the Divine Liturgies of Saints Basil, Gregory, and Cyril, *written in English, Coptic (middle), and Arabic.*

Even when the French occupied Egypt in 1798, followed by the British in the nineteenth century, most Copts still suffered as a result of their minority status. Some educated Copts were given privileged positions by the French and British, but most did not benefit. Instead of receiving support from the ostensibly Christian colonizers, they got the short end of the proverbial stick from imperialists more interested in appeasing the Egyptian Muslim majority than in helping fellow Christians. To curry favor with the majority, for instance, Napoleon Bonaparte declared that he recognized Mohammed as a prophet. Under the British, Lord Cramer's administration was so unsympathetic to the Copts that in 1911 they convened a national congress in Asyut to voice their grievances.[35]

In sum, this past is prologue to the modern story of the Copts in North America. The historical record reveals how the Copts came to speak Arabic, while still revering the Coptic script, and how they remained Christian despite a seemingly endless onslaught of persecution at the hands of their Muslim counterparts. So when the window of opportunity finally opened in the second half of the twentieth century, Copts began emigrating abroad in significant numbers, and the Coptic diaspora grew.

Forced Migration

n 1963 Edward Wakin noted the emerging Coptic emigration from Egypt: "The attachment of Copts to their Egyptian homeland is dramatized in the small-scale diaspora of the young, the educated, and the qualified who have begun to leave Egypt. They leave with reluctance, talking not of greener pastures elsewhere but of closed doors at home. Feeling deprived of the traditional Coptic right to market their skills at a reasonable price, they turn to the last resort of departure and dispersion."[36] Nearly a quarter of a century later, Pope Shenouda III wrote in a similar tone of Coptic emigration from Egypt: "The Copts as a community were sedentary by nature and upbringing. They loved the land of their birth and were averse to migration to other countries throughout their long history. The idea of moving from their ancestral home to a new milieu in search of better opportunities dawned upon them only recently, after the middle of the twentieth century, when they began under various economic and social influences to seek other opportunities abroad."[37] While these analyses are, undoubtedly, accurate, they gloss over the intensity of the economic and political push forces existent in modern Egypt. Such genteel accounts do not fully convey the dire straits so many Egyptian Copts face.

To be sure, the knife starts to hit the bone in the following story of a Copt who described his school experience growing up in Egypt: "We were a few

Christians, maybe around 8 or 9, and we took classes in religion and that is what made me learn a lot about Islam and memorize parts like Ayat al-Kursi and things like that. I still remember them. When we listened to the ayaat [verses], there was no difference that I am a Christian or a Muslim—the students, all of them had to memorize the ayaat that they were given in class. They told us that those who do not know the Qur'an, do not know the Arabic language well. This made me dislike the Arabic language. . . . This went against my self-esteem."[38] Such denigrating stories start to uncover the psychological trauma experienced by the minority Copts, but the real nature of their persecution in Egypt is best laid bare by remembering the victims who lost more than just their dignity.

John H. Watson correctly notes that the Egyptian government has failed the Copts in what is now a desperate and complicated situation, as illustrated by the following sampling of bloody events since the mid-1990s: "On 11 March 1994 two monks and three laymen were shot dead in the gateway to Al-Muh-harraq monastery. *Al-Gemaat el-Islamiya* killed two Christians on 31 July 1996 for refusing to pay protection money. In February 1996 eight Christians were killed in a gun attack on the church at Esbat al-Akbat. Twelve Copts were killed when *al-Gemaat el-Islamiya* stormed a church in Abu Quorqas on February 12, 1997. Later in the year . . . forty Copts were killed in Minya province, some faces deliberately disfigured with the backs of spades."[39] Such graphic reports, while disturbing and discomfiting, keep pouring out of Egypt.

In the Coptic Orthodox Christian village of Al-Kosheh, about 250 miles south of Cairo, Egypt, the new millennium got off to a bloody start. The main church building was draped in black as villagers grieved for the twenty Christians—including women and children—and one Muslim who died violent deaths in a January 2, 2000, shootout fueled by tensions between Muslims and Christians. Regarding the tragic event, Coptic Bishop Marcos commented that "[our] main problem is the poisoned climate between Muslims and Christians among large parts of the population. . . . We should not neglect this, but deal with it. After all, Christians only have a future in Egypt if Muslims and Christians live together in harmony, and we should work towards that end."[40] Sadly, the specter of religious extremism makes it increasingly difficult for Coptic Christians to live in Egypt.

In the course of my research, at the end of an interview with a respected elder of St. Mark Church, I was gently advised not to dwell on the Muslim-

Boutros Boutros-Ghali

Former United Nations Secretary-General Boutros Boutros-Ghali was born into a Coptic Christian family in Cairo, Egypt, on November 14, 1922. He graduated from Cairo University in 1946, earned a Ph.D. in international law from the University of Paris in 1949, studied at Columbia University on a Fulbright scholarship in 1954–55, and served as minister of state for foreign affairs in Egypt from 1977 to 1991. In the following excerpt from his memoir *Unvanquished: A U.S.-U.N. Saga* (1999), Boutros-Ghali describes his ascent toward the United Nations' top post:

> In May 1991, as we flew over the Mediterranean from Cairo to Paris, Egyptian President Hosni Mubarak told me he was going to promote me to vice-prime minister for foreign affairs. 'And, Boutros, since you love to work, I will also give you the post of minister of emigration, a ministry which needs to be gotten under control.' The ministry for emigration was responsible for more than 3 million Egyptian émigrés in the Arab world, Europe, Australia, Canada, and the United States. . . . While representing [Mubarak] at the June 1991 summit of the Organization of African Unity (OAU) in Abuja, Nigeria, the post of UN secretary-general was raised in a closed meeting of leaders, for it was 'Africa's turn' to select someone for the job.

Beginning on January 1, 1992, Boutros-Ghali served one five-year term as secretary-general of the United Nations. One of the most recognized Copts in the world, this diplomat, politician, and author's writings include *An Agenda for Peace* (1995) and *Egypt's Road to Jerusalem* (1997).

Christian strife in Egypt. It might reflect poorly on the Coptic community and, besides, who wants to focus on such fearsome problems? Unfortunately, it is a pressing human rights issue that cannot be ignored, and it plays a significant and unique role in the story of Coptic immigration to Michigan. At the same time, a few caveats should be mentioned. There are many counterexamples that soften the conceivably intolerant image of Egypt's Muslim population.

On the one hand, the majority of Egypt's Muslims are moderate and peaceable, and they abhor the violence perpetrated by an unrepresentative crew of religious extremists. Officially, Copts in Egypt are not classified as a minority—as Jews, Greeks, and Armenians are—because they are seen as ancient and original inhabitants of Egypt. Further, Article 46 of the Egyptian Constitution guarantees freedom of religious worship and practice.[41] A conciliatory step was made in 2003 by President Hosni Mubarak, who decreed that Christmas would henceforth be a national holiday, marking the first time that the Christian holiday has been officially recognized in modern Egypt. The official line is that Christian and Muslim Egyptians are coequals sharing cultural values and customs as well as a common Egyptian national identity. The great exemplar of this image of inclusiveness is Boutros Boutros-Ghali, a Copt who represented Egypt not only in the upper levels of national government, but also as secretary-general of the United Nations.

On the other hand, it is curious to note that, while Boutros-Ghali managed to rise to the top of the United Nations, he probably could never have become president of Egypt. Islam is the state religion of Egypt, and legislation is dictated by Islamic law,[42] some of which—to my mind, at least—is not only patriarchal and discriminatory, but also misogynist. For example, marriages between Muslim women and Christian men are not legally recognized, although a Muslim man may officially marry a Christian woman. It is illegal for a Muslim to convert to Christianity, although the reverse is allowed. Christians are forced to take off Fridays, the Muslim day of rest, but must work (or study, as the case may be) on Sunday.[43] The list of discriminatory transgressions is so long that it is little wonder Copts are prone to emigration.

Immigrating to Michigan

The Coptic community in North America and in the state of Michigan has come a long way in a rather short period of time. Indeed, it has grown exponentially since the 1960s. The first identifiable, yet relatively small, wave of Coptic immigrants arrived in the United States after implementation of the 1965 Immigration Act. A marked departure from the 1924 National Origins Act, which restricted the number of non-European immigrants entering the United States, the 1965 law was a product of the civil rights movement that transformed the ethnic makeup of immigrants entering the country. Coincidentally, fundamental change in American immigration law came at a time of political turmoil in Egypt. Following a military defeat by Israel in the 1967 Arab-Israeli War (or Six Days' War), Egypt suffered an economic crisis, diminished governmental legitimacy under President Gamal Abdel Nasser, and civil unrest. This combination of near-simultaneous events in Egypt and the United States led to an in increase in Coptic immigration to America.

Prior to 1965, there were relatively few Copts in the United States. The now defunct U.S. Immigration and Naturalization Service (INS)[44] reported that fewer than fifteen thousand Egyptians (of all religions, including Christians) immigrated to the United States in the decade from 1967 to 1976.[45] As noted earlier, they settled in America's biggest cities, such as New York, Detroit, and Los Angeles, the latter being particularly attractive because its warm Mediterranean-like climate resembles that of Egypt.[46] It was not until September 1970 that the first Coptic priest (Father Gabriel Abdelsayed) was appointed by the Coptic Orthodox Church in Egypt to lead a congregation in the United States (in Jersey City, New Jersey).

In the 1960s and early 1970s there were very few Copts in Michigan, hardly a community to speak of, and the early settlers who came were, for the most part, students and young professionals. Some came to pursue graduate degrees in engineering at the University of Michigan and Wayne State University, while others came to pursue professional careers in medicine, or specifically to work in the Detroit auto industry. Perhaps 30 to 40 percent of the early Coptic immigrants were single men in their twenties, who immigrated alone and later (if they were married) brought their wives and children to America.[47] Some married American women after they arrived in the United States. Still others immigrated via Europe, in particular Great Britain, a pattern explained by the colonial ties that exist between the Egyptians and the British.

An example of this circuitous migration route and motivation for leaving Egypt is provided by Joanne Aneese, who explains: "My husband came to Michigan from London where he had lived for ten years (originally from Egypt). He and I married approximately four years later. He left Egypt originally because he was disillusioned with the state of affairs in Egypt and wanted a different life."[48] This sentiment is echoed by many Copts in Michigan. In Egypt, a lack of opportunity combines with religious persecution to form a powerful dyadic push force. Michigan represents an equally powerful pull force, as economic and religious freedoms are at the heart of American political philosophy.

Two early Coptic immigrants, Dr. Anis Milad and Dr. Roushdy Boulos, are still active in St. Mark Church and were gracious enough to sit down with me and help piece together how the Coptic community emerged and evolved in the 1960s and 1970s. Dr. Anis Milad remembers how, in the fall of 1963, a group of about ten Copts in the Detroit area gathered for the first time to celebrate the liturgy. Led by Bishop Samuel, at the time visiting the United States to attend a meeting of the World Council of Churches, they congregated in one of their homes, prayed together, took communion, and made the best of their humble, living room service. An earlier researcher of the Copts in Michigan adds, in a similar vein, that, "Dr. Samir Ragheb, a physician who immigrated to the United States before Nasser came to power in Egypt, remembers a priest coming from Toronto about once a month to perform the liturgy in people's homes prior to 1967."[49] This priest was a man named Father Marqus Elias, who was appointed during the tenure of Pope Cyril VI (1959–71) to lead the first North American Coptic congregation (consisting of an original flock of thirty-six Coptic families) in Toronto, Canada.[50]

Dr. Roushdy Boulos, now retired, first came to the United States as a student. After two-and-a-half years of studying in New York, he returned to Egypt to marry, and then returned to America and settled for good in Detroit. Both Drs. Boulos and Milad list economics, a lack of opportunities, and religious oppression as reasons for leaving Egypt for America. To their knowledge, there were only about ten Coptic families in Detroit in the late 1960s, and because there was no Coptic church to go to, they would sometimes attend local Syrian or Antiochian churches. Then the small group of families took to holding their services in St. James Lutheran Church (in Detroit), which they rented. The first Coptic priest to lead a congregation in Detroit was Father Mikhail Melika, who served until 1977 and then returned to Egypt.[51] He was followed by Father Roufail Michail, who passed away in 1998. The two priests currently serving St. Mark Church are Father Mina Essak (since 1991) and Father Maximus Habib (since 2001). Both say they are waiting and praying that a third priest will one day join them.

As Father Mina tells it, the placement of St. Mark Church at 3603 Livernois Road in Troy, a northern suburb of Detroit, was providential. He recalls that, back in the mid-1970s, when he used to drive regularly from Chicago to Detroit to serve the community as a deacon, Troy seemed like a near-wilderness. One day Father Melika was driving by and noticed an advertisement, hidden among the trees, for a wooded parcel of land that was for sale. This, Father Melika believed, was a sign indicating where St. Mark Church should be built; destined by God, the church would be like Noah's Ark, save the flock, sail through the waves of the world and across the water to the harbor of salvation. The plot of nine acres of land was purchased in 1976 for $37,000.

Building St. Mark Church

The cornerstone of St. Mark Church was laid by Pope Shenouda III himself on May 1, 1977, during his two-month tour of the United States and Canada.

The first liturgy was celebrated in the new church nearly two years later, on May 8, 1979, the Feast Day of St. Mark the Evangelist. Additions to St. Mark Church were made in 1984, and again in 1988–89, when the north and south communion rooms were completed.

In many ways St. Mark Church is a crowning achievement of Michigan's Coptic community. It is the physical manifestation of the community's ethnic and religious identity, announcing to passersby on Livernois Road that there is a Coptic presence in Troy. It is, however, easy to whiz by in your car, as most people seem to do, and altogether miss the charming, modest church. Moreover, on the exact opposite side of the road is a cavernous, insipid edifice called Zion Christian Church, its massive parking lot and silver dome indicating that its tribe must be large. In stark contrast to its big Protestant neighbor, St. Mark Church, with its stained glass windows, Orthodox cross, and arched roof, seems small, quaint, and full of old-world character.

Over the years it became clear that St. Mark Church was, in fact, too small for the growing Coptic community. In need of more space and larger facilities, the congregation expanded. A school was built along with another, larger church called St. Mary and St. Philopater Coptic Orthodox Church (referred to simply as St. Mary Church). Pope Shenouda III again came to Troy on August 21, 2003, to personally open the new school. On that occasion a crowd of about three hundred exuberant congregants gathered round, some lucky enough to bow and kiss the hand of the Pope, who declared, "We have to care for our children. A church without youth is a church without a future. . . . If we don't look after them the devil may come and say 'I'll care for them.'"[52] From this vantage point, the stakes are, indeed, high.

The school consists of St. Mary's Child Development Center and St. Mark Christian Academy. The Child Development Center accepts infants, toddlers, and preschoolers up to five years old, and is open from 7:00 A.M. until 6:00 P.M. daily. A summer camp program is available as well, costing $400 per week for toddlers and $350 per week for preschoolers. The Christian Academy is for kindergartners and first-, second-, and third-grade students. Both are open to children of all faiths and cultures, but have a mission dedicated to providing an education with "Christian values" in a "Christian Orthodox environment." In addition to the usual subjects of English, math, science, and social studies, students at St. Mark Christian Academy learn the

St. Mark Coptic Orthodox Church in Troy, Michigan. St. Mary and St. Philopater Coptic Orthodox Church is located directly behind St. Mark. Courtesy of Eliot Dickinson.

Pope Shenouda III officially opening St. Mary's Child Development Center on August 21, 2003. Courtesy of Soli Soliman.

Father Mina Essak (center left), *Father Maximus Habib* (center right) *and members of the church celebrate the end of phase one of the construction of St. Mary and St. Philopater Coptic Orthodox Church. Courtesy of Soli Soliman.*

rudiments of the Coptic language and script. As one would expect at a private elementary school, it is small but active. A short yellow bus picks up children who need rides to school, uniforms are worn, and parents are involved in field trips, class parties, open houses, and potluck meetings.

St. Mary Church is located directly behind St. Mark Church, about one hundred yards away. Following its completion in 2006, nearly eight hundred congregants celebrated Christmas (on the Julian calendar) there for the first time on January 7, 2007. On that occasion Father Mina exclaimed, "We're really rejoicing this week, because this will be the first liturgy we've ever had inside our new $5-million church. Until now, we've been using space in the foyer of our new church, getting everything ready in the main part of the church. Now, we finally get to go inside."[53]

All of this construction, growth, and youthful activity is a manifestation of a vibrant community. Compared to the first humble gathering of Copts in the early 1960s, it becomes clear just how far Michigan's Coptic community has come. Contrasted with the religious persecution and grinding poverty found in Upper Egypt, the Coptic Church in Troy signals not just freedom, but opportunity and opulence. The building of schools and a larger church is an indication that the Coptic community is doing quite well. However, this growth did not happen by accident. It is the life's work of ambitious and talented people like Dr. Anis Milad, who wears many hats in the Coptic community: founding settler, medical doctor, Coptic youth convention leader, and church spokesperson. It is also the work of Father Mina, who serves tirelessly and, as if his many duties were not enough to fill his day, is also superintendent of the St. Mark Academy School Board. It is also the result of the efforts of Father Maximus, who is not only principal of the school, but is also known to drive the school bus in emergency situations. These are but a few of the many industrious, charitable people who form the backbone of the community.

A Welcoming Social Network

Aiding the pattern of settlement in Michigan, primarily in the Detroit area, is a vibrant social network that helps newcomers integrate into American society. Many Copts speak openly and warmly about their concerted efforts to be welcoming hosts to new arrivals, as well as their desire to facilitate Coptic emigration from Egypt by acting as official hosts for new immigrants. Once Copts arrive in Michigan, they are taken in by the established socioreligious network built around St. Mark Church and its extension, St. Mary Church, where they are helped with such practical necessities as finding a job, learning English, buying a car, and finding suitable living accommodations.

New immigrants also gravitate toward St. Mark Church for the sense of social and psychological belonging, for it is there that friends and family gather to feel connected to one another, and where members of the church help new arrivals adjust to a new way of life. One member of St. Mark Church, Joanne Aneese, described her family's experience this way: "The congregation has many 'groups' of people that have jelled together due to similar backgrounds, ideals, goals, likes, and dislikes. For example, when my husband's best friend from Egypt (they were in college together in Cairo) came to the States, he was living in Texas. My husband got him a job here in Michigan and that was the beginning of our group; then through other gatherings we gained families and grew. Also, our children made friends in Sunday school and that brought the adults together so that the kids can be together."[54] This type of social network strengthens the existing bonds connecting the Coptic community and explains why new arrivals settle in Detroit rather than other regions of the United States where there is not a large Coptic presence. If there is a law of migration, it is that once social networks and patterns of settlement are firmly established, they are likely to persist, mature, and reinforce the ties between the sending and receiving countries.

St. Mark Church is the hub of activity for Copts in the Detroit area, as well as the entire state, and its role cannot be overemphasized. It is where the "Seven Major Feasts" (Christmas, Epiphany, Easter, Palm Sunday, Pentecost, Ascension, and Annunciation), the "Seven Minor Feasts" (Circumcision of our Lord, Entrance into the Temple, Entrance into Egypt, Wedding of Cana, Transfiguration, Holy Thursday, and Thomas Sunday), and various other special holidays (such as Great Lent, Fast of Ninevah, Good Friday, Christmas Fast, Apostle's Feast, and St. Mary's Fast) are celebrated. Moreover, the church is not just where Copts gather to worship; it provides an all-important nexus between the religious and social—and, to a lesser extent, economic and political—components of the community. It organizes countless activities for members of all ages. Senior citizens meet on the last Friday of every month for an Arabic-speaking Bible study session. Saturday hymns classes are held in English and Arabic.[55] The St. Mina Retreat Center in the northern Michigan town of Mio holds regular gatherings and spiritual retreats for members of the Coptic community and the general public. Lastly, there are regular picnics for the youth, for "graduates" in their twenties, for families, and for the elderly, which provide opportunities for these respective groups to gather, socialize, network, play, meet, and court each other.

As some members of St. Mark see it, the church is in many ways an extension of the family: "We are very much involved with the Coptic community. Most of our friends and children's friends are Copts and we are very much involved in the church. Through our church friends we have a pseudo-family; we gather for Thanksgiving, Christmas, and Easter dinner, as well as numerous times visiting back and forth throughout the year. Our children have a safe haven in the church and with their church friends. My kids have found that their church friends are the ones that are there for them through thick and thin and the kids are very supportive of each other."[56] St. Mark Church and the activities it sponsors help create a social space in which to interact, thereby inculcating values, socializing the young into the community, and fostering the growth of the next generation of Copts.

Building community spirit at the St. Mina Retreat Center in Mio, Michigan. Courtesy of Soli Soliman.

St. Mina Retreat in Mio, Michigan

Whereas the great Coptic "Desert Fathers" of nearly 1,500 years ago (e.g., St. Makarios, St. Moses the Black, St. Mina the Wondrous) went into the Egyptian desert monasteries to seek spiritual peace, modern-day pilgrims can trek to the St. Mina Retreat Center in the northern town of Mio (located in the upper middle finger of the Lower Peninsula "hand map" known to all Michiganders). Michigan's equivalent of the Egyptian desert monastery is, however, surrounded by forests and ponds and is snow covered in the winter. Nonetheless, it offers people of all faiths, or none, a serene escape from the rat race of modern society. In addition to fresh air and solitude, the completed facility will include dormitory rooms, kitchen amenities, and a chapel. Pets, mini-skirts, smoking, drugs, and alcohol are not allowed, and quiet hours begin at 8:00 P.M. Guests are asked to bring sheets, toiletries, their Bible, and their Agpeya (The Coptic Orthodox "Book of Hours"), and to leave behind their portable televisions and DVD/CD players.

Joanne Aneese explains further: "In addition to congregating at the church for Bible study, etc., they also use it as a place to meet to go somewhere else. Throughout the years we have been part of Vacation Bible Study, Orthodox Basketball League, and Kids Camp (eight- to twelve-year-olds are taken on a four-day campout). At first, my kids were part of these activities as participants and I helped as a co-leader in some capacity. Now they are able to be coaches, leaders, and junior leaders themselves and are there to support the younger generation in these activities."[57] A concentration on healthy and constructive activities for the youth is, in part, a necessity of childrearing. But it has also to do with propagation of the Coptic community as a whole, for virtually every ethno-religious immigrant group has its eye on posterity and collective survival.

The Coptic Community

Despite being an oppressed minority in Egypt, Copts have traditionally been prominent among the major professions, such as engineering, medicine, law, and education. Since it was the skilled and educated who were most easily able to emigrate from Egypt from the late 1960s onward, the Coptic community in Michigan is generally an educated lot. It is easy to conclude that Michigan has benefited enormously from this brain drain, but it is harder to capture in a nutshell the professional characteristics of the Coptic community, or any community, without making broad generalizations. Nevertheless, a general outline can be discerned in accordance with Mansour Sidhom's observation in the early 1980s that, "since the belief in getting a good education is strong in the Coptic community, most Copts in Michigan are medical doctors or college or university professors."[58] This statement is, I believe, more than just vainglorious hyperbole.

In my conversations with members of the Coptic community, both young and old, I frequently heard such statements as: "I got my engineering degree and then . . . I worked for some years as an engineer," or "I'm studying engineering at Wayne State University." Father Mina and Father Maximus are role models as well as examples of this professional inclination. For instance, Father Mina explained, "I came here in 1974 as an engineer. I graduated from the college of engineering at Assiut University in Upper Egypt with a bachelor's degree in mechanical engineering in 1967."[59] When I asked him why Copts move to Michigan, of all places, and not sunny California, he responded: "It's mainly the auto industry. A lot of us who come have degrees in engineering, accounting, or medicine. Engineers, they have a lot of work in the auto industry; also, through the hospitals here, medical doctors have found employment. And some other businesses were flourishing here so they found work."[60] Similarly, Father Maximus said, "I came in March of 1991 as a structural engineer, since I used to work for a construction company back home. We came in March, and I started studying for a Masters degree to find a job as an engineer, because the market is very slow. So I started at Wayne State and I took the Masters degree in 1995. I used to take just one class a semester, because I have a family—my wife Nancy and at the time one kid. She used to study to get her license as a medical doctor."[61] Such a refrain is enough to leave the impression that all Copts are either engineers or doctors.

Of course, not everyone is or can be a highly skilled professional, and Copts do all manner of things for a living. Some are wealthy general medical practitioners, gynecologists, neurologists, dentists, and accountants; others are middle-class professors, educators, small business owners, nurses, realtors, construction workers, undertakers, and lawyers; still others are just scraping by financially, living at or below the poverty line. Members of the community do say, however, that Copts arriving today are different from their counterparts a generation ago, as there are now fewer with professional degrees and more who are uneducated. This recent phenomenon is, to some extent, explained by the fact that global telecommunications and jet-age travel have combined to make it easier for less educated Copts to make their way out of Egypt. Whereas the thought of actually immigrating to Detroit might never have entered the sphere of thinking of a semi-literate Egyptian in 1965, it is surely more than just a dreamy idea to many youngsters today who communicate via email with their cousins in America.

Assimilation

The Copts with whom I spoke all agreed that arranged marriages are a thing of the past and do not happen in Michigan. They point out that there are ample ways for young Copts to get to know each other, and courting is facilitated through St. Mark Church. However, one notes an occasional hint of tension between the old-world expectations of the immigrant generation and new-world freedom of American-born children, as illustrated in the following experience of a young Copt:

> The Bishop . . . Anba Antonius Markos . . . was saying at a convention that I went to, the Midwest Coptic Orthodox Youth Convention, that happens in some of the colleges around here . . . he was frowning upon it. He said we should . . . intermarry, marry within our own culture, to bring up our kids the right way. Obviously, we didn't buy into that because we should be able to marry who we want and bring people into the church, which was brought up in the convention . . . by a guy who brought his American girlfriend. But the Bishop's view, or the way I interpreted it at least, was that we . . . should use our own resources to multiply and make people that are all the same as us so that we don't deviate from the correct path. . . . It would be easier to keep the same traditions and values, if you come from a similar background.[62]

I asked Father Mina about the issue of assimilation and about the number of Copts who currently intermarry with native-born Americans not of Egyptian descent. He guessed that approximately four of the ten marriages occurring in the spring and summer of 2007 were mixed; then he paused, thought about the upcoming summer, and, counting deliberately on his fingers, revised his estimate upward to an even 50 percent. He also noted that, in order to be married in the Coptic Orthodox Church, non-Coptic partners must join the church or an affiliated member of the Oriental Orthodox Churches.

Assimilation into American society inevitably means that Copts will intermarry with Americans of other denominations, faiths, and ethnicities, and the succeeding children born in Michigan will be increasingly Americanized. Following the typical pattern of past immigrant groups in the United States, the American-born children will speak English with an American accent, take on American customs, and join the American melting pot, or salad bowl, or kaleidoscope. That is to say, they will become part of the fabric of America's multicultural, ethnically pluralist society.

The Midwest Coptic Orthodox Youth Convention

Midwest Coptic Orthodox Youth Conventions (MCOYC) have been held annually since 1984 in various locations across the Midwest, for example at Eastern Michigan University in Ypsilanti and Hope College in Holland. In July 2007 the 24th annual MCOYC was held at Bowling Green State University in Bowling Green, Ohio. Coptic youths from around the Midwest and Canada attend the week-long conventions, consisting of Bible study, lectures, and social activities, along with local Coptic priests and bishops. The 1997 MCOYC in Ypsilanti was led, for example, by Fathers Mikhail Mikhail, Rewis Awadalla, Samuel Thabet, Mina Essak, Roufail Michail, Bishoy Fahmy, Guirguis Ghobrial, and Isaac Tanious. The Hope College office of public relations announced in the summer of 1998 that about two hundred would attend the Coptic Orthodox Young Adult Convention (July 23–26, 1998) and Coptic Orthodox Youth Convention (July 27–31, 1998). A decade after hosting the MCOYC at Hope College, administrators and faculty still vividly remember the youthful delegates, black-clad and bearded priests, and pungent buckets of swinging incense used during the "raising of the incense" in the campus's Dimnent Chapel.

Coptic Names

While conducting field research in the hyperpluralist suburbs of Detroit, where Orthodox churches of all stripes can be found seemingly at every corner, I was fortunate enough to meet an Ethiopian priest of the Ethiopian Orthodox Tewahedo Church, which is in communion with the Coptic Orthodox Church (See Appendix 3: Ethiopian Coptic Christians).[63] One of the first topics in the course of our introductory small talk dealt with the meanings of both our names. He explained that his name, Zelalem, meant "forever." This ice-breaking chitchat revealed the cultural salience of first and last names among Coptic Christians, both Egyptian and Ethiopian.

Names are distinctive indicators of ethnic and religious identity. They are important in that they announce not only who a person is, but to which ethno-religious group he or she belongs. Names also have deep symbolic meaning, as they reflect Coptic history. For example, some names commonly used by Copts are of pharaonic origin (such as Anubis); some are Coptic (Bishoi), and some are both Coptic and pharaonic (Mina). Others are of Greek (Dimitri), Latin (Fiktur), Hebrew (Gabra), or Arabic (Farah) origin.[64] Coptic names also commonly have idiosyncratic meanings. The name Andarawus (Andrew) is of Coptic-Greek origin and means "manhood," while the Arabic Abd-al-Masih means "servant of Christ," and the Hebrew-Aramaic Gabra means "strong man." To mention but one example, the name of one of the most famous of all Copts, former United Nations secretary-general Boutros Boutros-Ghali, is derived from the Coptic-Greek Boutros (Peter) and Arabic Ghali (dear, or costly). The secretary-general's very name marked him as a characteristic representative of Egypt during his tenure on the world stage.

However, with Muslim-Christian tensions running high in Egypt, some Egyptian Copts are opting for Arabic names commonly used by both Copts and Muslims, such as Adel (just) and Mansur (the victorious one). In Michigan, Copts feel no pressure to conceal their Christianity, and children are frequently given common biblical names, such as Christina and Matthew. Moreover, judging by anecdotal evidence, Mark and Mary are among the most popular names of children and edifices, as exemplified by the names of St. Mark Church and St. Mary Church in Troy.

Persecution and Solidarity

Persecution of Egypt's Copts, as described in detail earlier, acts as a powerful push force and cause of emigration. In the United States, it also functions as an emotional unifying issue, which, in turn, has resulted in political mobilization and even radicalization. Mansour Sidhom's monthly newsletter, the *Peace News,* for example, was a provocative wellspring of agitation and propaganda in the Detroit Coptic community in the late 1970s and 1980s.

On a practical political level, the Coptic community in America currently lobbies its congressional representatives to put pressure on the Egyptian government to improve the treatment and protection of Copts there. It is possible that Egypt's 2003 recognition of Christmas as a national holiday was a result of Coptic lobbying and pressure from the U.S. government.

Twenty-first-century technology, in particular the Internet, is used to urge Egypt to follow international human rights norms. For example, the

The *Peace News*

Writing about an ethno-religious group and attempting to capture fully the issues, problems, challenges, joys, and triumphs of the community can be a delicate task. The researcher must balance how he or she sees the community with how the community wishes to see itself. For example, I was told that the *Peace News* (or *Majallat al-salām* in Arabic), a monthly newsletter popular in the Michigan Coptic community in the late 1970s and 1980s, was not a credible source of information. Nothing could have so piqued my scholarly curiosity than this dismissal of the *Peace News*. Unfortunately, the obscure newsletter, which was published in Detroit and at one point sold as many as four thousand copies per month, is archived only at the Library of Congress in Washington, D.C., and nowhere—to my knowledge—in Michigan. This is an unfortunate lacuna that should be filled by one of the state's many great libraries.

The August 1985 edition of the *Peace News*, which is a cut-and-paste collection of sensational reports, includes "The Coptic Anthem: Forgive But Do Not Forget You Also Have a Right To Get Freedom, Equality, Justice And Respect To Live in Peace without Threat." The headlines read (without punctuation): "Implication of Applying the Koranic Code on the Christians in Egypt Racism and Genocide," and "Islamization by Force Jihad." If nothing else, the *Peace News* is a noteworthy artifact of agitprop from the early decades of the Coptic community in Michigan.

U.S. Copts Association Web site (*www.copts.com*) promotes the general interests of the global Coptic diaspora.[65] A large part of this promotion relies on raising international awareness of human rights abuses in Egypt. To this end, sensational reports on violence against Coptic Christians in Egypt are dispatched on a regular basis. Keen observers will find no shortage of descriptive articles on Coptic persecution in the American mainstream media, where headlines such as "The Silent Exodus: Extremist Landscape in Egypt Is Where Violence Takes Hold" are not uncommon.[66] In addition, a number of magazines, newsletters, and journals, such as *The Independent Copt, The Free Copts Magazine, Saint Mark Monthly Review, Coptic Church Review,* and *St. Shenouda Coptic Newsletter,* circulate in print and on the Internet and serve to inform and connect the various Coptic communities in both America and Egypt.

The Coptic Christian weekly newspaper *Watani* is explicit in its reporting, as illustrated in the following excerpt posted in May 2007 on the U.S. Copts Association Web site: "The repercussions of the sectarian violence which erupted on Friday 11 May in the village of Bemha in Ayaat, Giza, are still reverberating around. That fateful Friday, a mosque imam's call for jihad to defend Islam against the threat of the Christian villagers' intention to build a church, worked up a fanatic mob. Armed with white weapons [knives and daggers] and carrying kerosene flasks, roaring Islamic slogans, they marched onto the Christians' homes and property, attacking, looting, plundering, and burning. Ten Copts were injured and 70 houses set on fire."[67] The alarmist ring of the excerpt expresses the sense of frightful desperation experienced by many Copts in Egypt. Unfortunately, while Egyptian authorities officially decry attacks against Christians, they have been either unwilling or unable to quell the violence, which continues with disturbing regularity.

It is hard to extricate Coptic life in Michigan from politics in Egypt, especially among the immigrant generation. Copts are in Michigan largely because of the political push forces in Egypt, namely the overt oppression they face as a minority group. What happens in Egypt is on the minds of Copts in Michigan, who are more aware of Egyptian politics than ever before. Forces of globalization, such as satellite television (which broadcasts Egyptian news, soap operas, and sports into Michigan living rooms) and the World Wide Web have raised the consciousness of the Coptic diaspora to the extent that Copts in Detroit, London, Melbourne, and Cairo are increasingly interconnected.[68] Instantaneous and relatively cheap communication between the United States and Egypt insures that members of the Coptic community in Michigan are acutely aware of the persecution faced by their co-religionists in Egypt.

Sadly, there is only a limited amount that the Coptic community in Michigan can do to change the political status quo in Egypt. Lobbying Egyptian politicians on behalf of the Copts is rarely successful. In Father Mina's words, "It does not bring any fruits." Rather, Father Mina believes prayer is the most powerful tool in the face of political and religious persecution, and for inspiration points to the biblical passage "Blessed are they which are persecuted for righteousness' sake: for theirs is the kingdom of heaven."[69] From his

ecclesiastic vantage point, the suffering and persecution that the Copts in
Egypt have experienced since at least the seventh century A.D. is a blessing
from the Lord and a way to share Christ's pain. Persecution is part and parcel
of the history of the Coptic Orthodox Church in Egypt and an awakening call
for Christians to keep their faith and remain vigilant. Needless to say, this is
a quintessentially clerical view of the oppression, intimidation, harassment,
and violence that Copts face, but it is shared to a lesser degree by the laity in
both Michigan and Egypt.

The Liturgy

Father Mina and Father Maximus are extremely busy men. There is much
to do, every day of the week. On Sundays from 7:00 to 10:30 A.M. there is
a three-and-a-half-hour Arabic-language service in St. Mark Church. This
overlaps with the English service, held from 8:30 to 11:30 A.M. in the nearby
St. Mary Church. Generally speaking, Arabic-speaking immigrants, parents, and grandparents attend the earlier service, while their children and
grandchildren, and those who speak only English, attend the later service.
Additional services are held from 5:00 to 7:30 on Wednesday mornings, 7:00
to 10:00 on Thursday mornings, and 9:30 to 12:30 on Friday mornings. On
Monday evenings, starting (by appointment) at 7:00, Father Maximus hears
confession. Father Mina likewise hears confession on Tuesday evenings. On
the first, second, and third Saturdays of the month one of the two venerable
priests drives to Grand Rapids, Ann Arbor, and Lansing, respectively, to celebrate the Eucharist with congregants who live in the far reaches of the state.
Fathers Mina and Maximus also attend to and preside over a steady stream
of baptisms, confirmations, marriages, illnesses, funerals, and blessings of
all sorts. Their days are long, but they serve their flock with an evident and
inexhaustible passion.

Arguably the most important of the priests' duties is conducting the
Coptic liturgy, the celebration of the Eucharist. Lasting three hours or more,
the Coptic liturgy is not for the faint of heart; it requires stamina and concentration. Besides the addition of the English language, there appears to
be little difference in the way the liturgy is celebrated in Egypt and the way
it is celebrated in Michigan. Congregants in a position to know say that, if
anything, the services in Michigan are more traditional and conservative

Celebration of Easter in St. Mary Church. Men sit on the left, women on the right. Courtesy of Soli Soliman.

than in Egypt. In Father Maximus's words, "some people come here and tell us that our church is more spiritual and more strict than back in Egypt. We are trying to stay true to the core of our religion."[70]

One scholar wrote of the experience in Egypt: "The unifying function of the church is particularly evident at Sunday Mass. In their animated celebration of the changing of bread and wine into the divinity of Christ, the Copts fill the church with the tangibles of religious worship. Sight, sound, smell, touch are all involved as the congregation acts out membership in the group."[71] Richard R. Jones described the service at St. Mark Church in Troy this way: "Besides the overt religious significance, the symbols and rituals of the liturgy serve to communicate the solidarity of the group to the individual. The costuming, the ceremonial movements around the altar, the icons, the incense, the colored light, the hypnotic rhythm of the percussion instruments, the hymns, and the chanting are all elaborately coordinated in the Coptic liturgy."[72] Such are the services that occur in St. Mark Church and St. Mary Church on a daily and weekly basis.

The services held in Grand Rapids, Ann Arbor, and Lansing are similar, except on a smaller, more intense scale. On a brisk Saturday morning in Grand Rapids I joined about twenty Copts celebrating the liturgy in the rented basement of the International Fellowship Church on Kalamazoo Avenue. Father Maximus Habib leaves St. Mark Coptic Orthodox Church in Troy at the crack of dawn and drives across the state in order to start the liturgy at 8:30 A.M. Like Father Maximus, Copts from across Western Michigan—from Kalamazoo, Muskegon, Big Rapids, and Traverse City— drive great distances in the early morning hours for this opportunity to attend the Coptic service. From 8:30 to 9:00 A.M. Father Maximus, donned in his customary black robe, performs a preparatory ceremony called the "raising of the incense" while worshipers enter, taking their places among rows of chairs. An aisle in the middle of the makeshift pews separates the men and boys, who sit on the left, from the women and girls, who sit on the right. Most worshippers take their shoes off, and some women cover their heads with scarves in the Egyptian style.

Father Maximus is helped by a deacon and three young altar boys sitting at the front of the men's side. An older man chants and sings hymns in Arabic, followed directly by a younger man chanting in English, each complement- ing the other in a moving synthesis of the Arabic and English languages, and Egyptian and American cultures. When the liturgy starts at 9:00 A.M., Father Maximus puts on his white robe and hat with the distinctive Coptic Christian cross on the front. With the exception of two little girls who pass out white towels to cover each worshiper's mouth after taking communion, the liturgy is conducted entirely by men, an indication of the patriarchal structure of the Coptic Orthodox Church.

Plenty of pungent incense is used in the liturgy, which forms a thick cloud that dries the throat and eyes, leaving a sweet odor in the pages of the hymnbooks and in one's clothes. The haze nearly obscures the view in the room, and would surely set off the smoke detectors, were they not covered to prevent this. In the background is a row of fake tulips planted in a long rectangular box, a reminder that the liturgy is being celebrated in Western Michigan, the upper Middle West of America, in the basement of a rented Protestant church.[73] On the one hand it seems to emphasize how far from Egypt these congregants are, yet on the other it is also clear that they are very much at home.

The liturgy is noteworthy in that it is done at least half in Arabic, which makes it—despite the help of friendly men sharing their hymnbooks and pointing to the appropriate passages—all but unintelligible to the average

American visitor. Then, suddenly, the Lord's Prayer and other recognizable biblical passages are heard in English. Also notable is the way the alter boys kneel down and bend forward, prostrate on the floor, in the way Muslims do during prayer. Indeed, even the intonation of the Arab-language prayers and hymns of the Coptic liturgy sound remarkably similar to a Muslim prayer—a reminder of the Arabic and Islamic influence on Coptic Christianity.[74] Perhaps the most touching part of the service, literally and figuratively, is when Father Maximus comes around and places his hand on each person's forehead and, using his thumb, makes the sign of the cross. It inspires a sense of spirituality and connection to two thousand years of Coptic history, of which the liturgy is both a manifestation and a continuation.

Coptic Revival

Much has been written about the revival of both the Coptic Church and monasticism in modern Egypt. Otto F. A. Meinardus, for instance, writes that the "unprecedented revival of the Coptic Church toward the second half of the twentieth century is one of the great historical events of world Christianity."[75] Pope Shenouda III has played a central role in this renewal of the Coptic Church and its flock in and outside of Egypt. During his tenure as pope, for example, the number of bishops in the diaspora has grown from three in 1971 to nineteen in 2006, while the number of monks has likewise grown exponentially from 200 to 1,200 in roughly the same time period.[76] In the United States the number of Coptic churches rose from two in 1970 to forty-one in 1989.[77] Today there are approximately one hundred.

In addition to Pope Shenouda III's leadership, there are a number of interconnected reasons for this revival. The Copts in Egypt are responding to real persecution, perceived by many as an existential threat, which has produced a redoubled effort to strengthen the church as an institution, increase the sense of global connectedness among the Copts, and even teach and learn the Coptic language. This may, in some measure, also be a reaction to the parallel Islamic revival found in modern Egypt. At a time when Copts are facing increasing persecution in Egypt, the global Coptic community is burgeoning. Whereas building a new Coptic church in Egypt is a near impossibility due to bureaucratic red tape and Muslim antipathy (until 1998 it required presidential authorization), in Michigan it is an unproblematic matter of course.

Pope Shenouda III appears to be truly interested in the global diaspora and dedicated to the Coptic Church's global mission, as indicated by his repeated visits to Troy. He provides inspiration and is, in part, responsible for the growth of the Coptic community in Michigan. Where there was once a thicketed forest on Livernois Road in Troy, there are now two churches (St. Mark and St. Mary), a preschool (St. Mary's Child Development Center), and an elementary school (St. Mark Christian Academy) in which the next generation of Copts is being educated. In nearby Ann Arbor, plans are underway to buy land and build a new Coptic church, already tentatively named St. Mary Coptic Orthodox Church. Further, the St. Mina Retreat Center in Mio acts as Michigan's version of the Egyptian desert monastery, secluded far from the hustle and bustle of the maddening crowd. In total, these are manifestations of the global Coptic renewal.

An Evolving Identity

The terrorist attacks against the United States on September 11, 2001, had a perceptible impact on the Copts in Michigan. In the year following the attacks on the World Trade Towers and the Pentagon, the attitudes and behavior of some Americans toward people of Middle Eastern descent did, in fact, change. Since many Copts have typically Middle Eastern physical features (e.g., dark hair and complexion) and they usually speak Arabic, they are frequently taken to be Muslims. As a result, some in the Coptic community have felt the slings and arrows of post-9/11 xenophobia in the United States. On the whole, however, American intolerance toward Arab Americans has been relatively mild, and the Copts whom I interviewed all said that they have been treated well by their fellow Americans.

Father Mina, for instance, feels he has been treated fairly, but not in any special positive or negative way. However, he admits in his endearing way that he began ostentatiously flying the United States flag in front of his house in the wake of September 11, 2001, in order to express his patriotism and identity as an American (see Appendix 1). The worst that he experienced was in the months following the terrorist attacks, when a small group of misguided and ignorant youths shouted at him to "go home." Compared to the open discrimination in Egypt, where Copts are often shut out of the best jobs and face serious religious persecution, such verbal insults seem relatively tame. Whereas Copts in Egypt are occasionally killed in religious strife, life in Michigan is characterized by high degrees of religious tolerance, social and economic opportunity, and freedom.

Christianity is a major component of Coptic identity, and both Father Mina and Father Maximus want people to see and know that they are Christian. To this end, both wear a black and white leather Coptic cross around their necks, dangling visibly on their chests for all to see. Yet even this does not always achieve the desired effect, as they are still occasionally mistaken for Muslims. In the United States, where Christianity is the predominant religion, many Copts feel it is important to explicitly express their religious identity. It is as if they prefer to identify with American Christians, who make up the majority of the population, than to identify with Muslims—many of whom Americans suspect of religious extremism, or worse.[78]

The wars in Iraq and Afghanistan, widely perceived in the Muslim world to be wars against Islam, have not only exacerbated Muslim-Christian tensions in Egypt, but also heightened Coptic sensitivities in America. Coptic-Muslim relations in Michigan have remained without incident, thankfully, but there have been conflicts elsewhere. In Jersey City, New Jersey, home of the largest Coptic population in the country, tensions boiled over in January 2005 when a Coptic family of four was murdered. Many Copts suspected the perpetrators were Muslim and that the killings were an extension of the gruesome violence against Christians in Egypt.[79] While relations between Copts and Muslims in Detroit are peaceful, it is not inconceivable that problems could arise. It is also clear that Copts are eager to distance themselves from any association with Muslims, and especially Muslim extremism.

One perennial question regards whether Copts are Arabs. The answer is an equivocal, unsatisfying yes and no. Egyptian Copts are in most ways indistinguishable from Egyptian Muslims in culture and language, yet most do not identify themselves as Arabs, even though they speak Arabic and come from a country that defines itself as Arabic (i.e., the Arab Republic of Egypt, as it is officially known). Michigan Copts resist the Arab label mostly because it is widely equated with Islam; over the centuries Arab has come to mean Muslim, just as Coptic and Christian are inextricably linked in the popular imagination and in everyday parlance.

In Michigan, those who self-identify as Arabs also tend not to see the Copts as such. The Arab American National Museum in Dearborn, for example, makes only passing reference to the Copts. Rosina J. Hassoun's *Arab Americans in Michigan*—part of the Discovering the Peoples of Michigan series—makes not a single reference to the Copts. Nevertheless, technically speaking and in a sociological sense, Copts are Arabs, or Arab Christians, as they speak Arabic and have been culturally Arabized. Nabeel Abraham and Andrew Shryock's *Arab Detroit: From Margin to Mainstream* includes an insightful chapter on Egyptian Copts in Detroit.[80]

An inescapable element of Coptic life in both Egypt and Michigan relates to being a minority. In his 1963 classic, for example, Edward Wakin calls the Copts *A Lonely Minority*. Immigration to Michigan has altered the status of the Copts so that they are neither oppressed nor necessarily lonely, but they are still a minority of sorts. As one Copt in Detroit put it, "the Copts are a subset of the Egyptian population. The Egyptian population's mainly composed of Muslims. So, when you say you're Egyptian, people assume you are from the land of the pyramids and a Muslim. So, they're wrong on their assumption, 'cause I'm in the minority. I am a minority amongst a minority. Egyptians in the United States are a minority to begin with, and I am a subset of that."[81] This excerpt is revealing in that it expresses an acute awareness of being associated with Muslims as well as being a double minority. At the same time, a notable aspect of the Coptic immigrant experience is that Copts in the United States remain an ethnic minority but are no longer a religious minority. They suddenly become members of the larger Christian majority, as over 80 percent of the United States population self-identifies as Christian.[82]

I will never forget how, as I sat drinking coffee as a guest in her living room, one Coptic woman expressed her Christianity. With a proud smile beaming across her face, she held up her hand and revealed a small tattooed cross on the inside of her right wrist. This widespread practice among devout Christians is a powerful symbol and identifying mark; it is an unmistakable, explicit, permanent expression of their religion, and some also believe it wards off evil spirits and disease. As an early father of the Coptic Church put it, "where the seal of the cross is, the wickedness of Satan hath no power to do harm."[83] The practice of tattooing is becoming less popular, especially in Egypt, but one Copt with whom I spoke estimated that between 10 and 20 percent of young Copts in the United States still get a tattooed cross on the inside of their right wrist.

In sum, Coptic identity is at once complex, multidimensional, and even contradictory. Copts in Michigan hold up the Coptic language as a cherished jewel of their inheritance, but it is in practice a dead language. Many speak Arabic, but reject being identified as Arab. Their historical consciousness is that of an oppressed minority in Egypt, but in Michigan the tables are turned, as Copts find themselves among an American population that is overwhelmingly Christian. At the end of the day, Copts in Michigan are at once any combination of Coptic, Christian, secular, Arabic, Western, African, Egyptian, American, and Michigander. They are forging, with a burst of hybrid vigor, their own Coptic-American-Michigander identity.

Conclusion

When European crusaders began journeying to the Holy Land in the eleventh century A.D. to wage war against Islam, it led to increased persecution of the Christian minorities in the Middle East—including the Copts in Egypt. An astounding parallel can be seen today, in a new millennium, resulting from the American invasions of Iraq and Afghanistan. The war in Iraq has not only led to immeasurable human suffering, carnage, and an untold number of deaths, it has also exacerbated Muslim-Christian tensions and intensified the maltreatment of Christians across the Muslim world in general, and of Copts in Egypt in particular.[84] Almost without exception, the Copts in Michigan with whom I spoke expressed grave concern, even pessimism, about the plight of their Christian brethren in Egypt. Few are as certain as their religious leaders that the persecution is a blessing or a welcomed test of their spiritual resolve. Rather, most see a bleak future for the Copts in Egypt, who make up the largest Christian minority in the Middle East. The general consensus is that the Coptic community in Egypt will not disappear, but that its size will decrease as a result of persecution, conversion to Islam, and forced emigration.

By contrast, the Coptic community in Michigan is, by all accounts, flourishing. The many Coptic engineers, medical doctors, dentists, accountants, and other professionals who have immigrated since the 1960s, mostly to the Detroit area, represent the best and the brightest new Michiganders. As regrettable as the phenomenon of global brain drain is, Egypt's loss appears to be Michigan's gain. The Copts have made a significant, welcomed, and positive socioeconomic contribution to the state. Moreover, guided ably by the good Fathers Mina Essak and Maximus Habib, the community is growing and the future looks promising. With an established social network firmly in place and a welcoming group of co-ethnics ready to receive Coptic immigrants from Egypt, the pattern of settlement established in the 1960s is likely to continue.

Immigrants often bring the political tensions of their homeland with them. While there is a discernable degree of long-distance nationalism among the Copts in Michigan, it is of the most benevolent kind.[85] Where Muslim-Christian tensions in Egypt are overwrought, sometimes resulting in hate crimes and murder, the two communities are peaceful here. America's ethnic diversity and relative tolerance of newcomers have ameliorated the ethno-religious passions found in North Africa and the Middle East. From the hyperpluralist suburbs of Detroit to the midsize cities and bucolic towns across the state of Michigan, the Copts live their lives not as a lonely minority, but as one among many.

An Interview with Father Mina Essak

Troy, April 20, 2007

On the warm spring afternoon of April 20, 2007, I interviewed Father Mina Essak at St. Mary Church in Troy, Michigan. With his black robe, distinctive beard, olive-colored skin, and pleasant demeanor, Father Mina is the classic picture of a Coptic priest. He is an intelligent, engaging man who is wholly committed to his work. Our interview lasted over two hours, during which Father Mina showed extraordinary patience and generosity. We sat together in the wooden pews of the empty and silent church, with a tape recorder between us, and had the following conversation.

Eliot Dickinson (ED): Perhaps you could tell me a little bit about yourself, where you are from, your life story.

Father Mina: I came here in 1974 as an engineer. I graduated from the college of engineering at Assuit University in Upper Egypt with a bachelor's degree in mechanical engineering in 1967. I was born in a small city called Edfu in Upper Egypt. I came to England first in 1973 and then I migrated to Chicago in April 1974. I stayed for three years there and then I came here and got married to my wife. And from 1977 until now roughly I am a resident of Michigan, except for a few years I traveled to other states to serve as a priest. I have been called to serve as a priest since 1991 at this church, and that's where I am.

ED: How did you end up coming to Michigan?

Father Mina: I came to Michigan first to help the priest in Chicago, Father Markos. He was serving the congregation here [in Detroit] because they had no priest, and I was helping him for about two years as a deacon. And later on he introduced me to the family of my wife, and after we got married I moved here.

ED: Why do other Copts move to Michigan?

Father Mina: It's mainly the auto industry. A lot of us who come have degrees in engineering, accounting, or medicine. Engineers, they have a lot of work in the auto industry; also, through the hospitals here, medical doctors have found employment. And some other businesses were flourishing here so they found work.

ED: When did the first Copts come to this area?

Father Mina: The first wave of immigration took place in 1967-68. I was among the first to come. That's when the United States opened the door for immigration so professionals from third world countries could come here. There are a few people who traveled here earlier than that, in the early sixties, but those are only a few. Some of them came to continue their education, some of them were doctors and had contracts to come and work here, but the majority of the immigrants started coming in late 1967 and early 1968.

ED: Were there specific push forces or reasons why you and other Copts left Egypt?

Father Mina: I left Egypt because I wanted to see what is outside. A lot of people are leaving Egypt now because America is very generous to the newcomers, and they are seeking opportunities for themselves and their children. And some are escaping persecution. There are persecutions still until now against Christians in Egypt so they are seeking chances to seek a better life and freedom of religion.

ED: Has the persecution in Egypt intensified over the last few years?

Father Mina: It goes up and down, but it has been consistent for the last few years. There are Christians being killed and churches being burned. People have been harassed, and we have lived with this for years.

ED: How do you keep in touch with Egypt now? How do others in the Coptic community keep in touch?

Father Mina: Mainly through the Internet now, and we have free communication with people in Egypt. A lot of people travel back and visit home every two or three years, depending on their economic status. And through phone conversations, and relatives come here in the summer and visit.

ED: How do you define a Copt?

Father Mina: The word "Copt" used to define an Egyptian, as opposed to a non-Egyptian or someone not living in Egypt. But lately, after the Islam invasion it is used to define the Christians of Egypt instead of all the Egyptians. A Copt is a very zealous Christian. They accept their faith from St. Mark, one of the disciples who preached Christianity in Egypt, and since that time Christianity flourished in Egypt. They are proud of their heritage. They are also proud that Egypt is the only land that the Lord visited. The land of Egypt is blessed by the visit of the Lord and Saint Mary and Saint Joseph. And we have many places where they stayed, which became monasteries and churches. A Copt is also a faithful Egyptian. We are faithful to our land, to our relatives, and a Copt is a courageous person, which is a fundamental characteristic of any Christian. We are not afraid, because the Lord is on our side. We try to say the truth. A Copt is very generous and very giving, and we open our doors to the newcomers who are new to the state, because we came once when nobody was around, and we don't want those newcomers to face the same situation. So we have to welcome those who are coming here so they don't have a hard time. As an ethnic group we try to cling to one another. We seek comfort in this, and the church is where we all gather.

ED: So would you define being a Copt mostly in religious terms, or also in ethnic terms? Who can be a Copt? Could I become a Copt?

Father Mina: Anybody who would like to convert to the Coptic Orthodox Church can become a Copt, even though they were not born in Egypt. We tend to give this title based on the heritage of the religion. So we are preaching Coptic Orthodox Christianity, and those who accept Christianity through our faith, they are considered Copts even though they are not by definition Egyptians.

ED: Could you possibly have an Arab Copt or a Muslim Copt?

Father Mina: Like I told you, Coptic nowadays became a way to identify Egyptians, but now after Egyptians migrated outside of Egypt the word became a little bit wider and includes all those who believe in the Coptic Orthodox faith. A Muslim could consider himself Coptic based on the old definition as a person living in Egypt.

ED: There are some African Americans who call themselves Copts because they identify with Moses the Black—what do you think of Americans, white or black, who say they are Copts?

Father Mina: I'm not sure of the relation between what they say or claim in regard to the definition of the word "Copt."

ED: Do you ever face discrimination here in Michigan, where people think you are Arab and don't realize you are Christian?

Father Mina: After 9/11 we faced this kind of treatment, but I refer to myself as a clergyman. The way they look at me wearing a black robe and a hat, they identify me with the way a terrorist looks. After 9/11 I was filling my car with gas at the gas station and a group of kids shouted at me "Go home!" So we could be mistakenly viewed as terrorists, among the Arabs, and treated differently. But lately things have quieted down, but it was very high after 9/11.

ED: Do you make sure to display your cross, so people can tell you are Christian?

Father Mina: Yes, this cross that I wear was a sign of humiliation when Islam came to Egypt. They used to make Christians wear a seven-pound heavy cross to distinguish them. We take it as a sign of glory, we are proud to carry the cross, and it is very essential for people to know that I am a Coptic Orthodox priest. Without a cross and a black robe they could easily mistake me for a rabbi. On more than one occasion, even with a cross, they call me rabbi (laughter).

ED: Can you describe your congregation here at St. Mark?

Father Mina: We have around 520 families here, mainly around where the church is in Troy. There are some satellite congregations in Ann Arbor, Lansing, and Grand Rapids. It used to be the church in Windsor [Canada] was part of here, before they got their own church and priest. Many of the congregation are professionals—engineers, accountants, doctors, and nurses. Now a good part of the congregation is newcomers, and some of them are not professionals but have a trade that they used to do back in

Egypt. So those who are established here are helping those who are new to find a job, get their Social Security, help them get a driver's license, find a used car. But the majority who are established here are professionals.

ED: Can you tell me about the children in the community and how they are assimilating into American life?

Father Mina: We have children here who were born in the 1960s and now they are adults and now they are professionals with families and babies and are doing well. So there is a second and third generation who are born here in the States, are mixed very well in the society. They speak the language without an accent, like I have. So you cannot distinguish them among any Americans at school or work. Except we would love to keep our heritage, not to separate us from the community, but to look at it as something very special that we would like to keep and give to the new generation. So we take the best from the society, and we take the best from our culture, and we mix it together and try to keep that. The idea of a school here was encouraged by His Holiness Pope Shenouda III. He encouraged all the priests throughout the world to have a Coptic school where the kids will go and receive the academic teaching at the highest level, learn the Coptic language that the Muslims prohibited us from using, and also learn about the church and their heritage. So they will be graduated from a school as healthy individuals, have been taught in a good Christian environment, be good members of society and members of the church.

ED: Are you concerned at all that through assimilation they will lose touch with their Coptic Egyptian roots?

Father Mina: Unfortunately it will happen in the future, because not all of them are visiting Egypt regularly. A lot of them are spending ten, fifteen years without even once visiting Egypt. So, yes, they might lose touch, but now with technology there are lots of Web sites about the Coptic language and inheritance. We get in touch, but not as we would like. For instance, my kids have not been to Egypt, and the eldest is around twenty-seven years old. We are trying to go next year, but so far we were not successful all those years.

ED: Is it difficult to go back, perhaps difficult to get a visa?

Father Mina: No, for an Egyptian born here as an American it is no problem getting a visa. If you have a family of three or four, the airline tickets play a major role. But staying there with relatives is very inexpensive. It is mainly the cost associated with flying.

ED: And what do the children here at the St. Mary School learn?

Father Mina: They have Coptic language classes for Coptic hymns, for church festivities. So they will learn very in-depth about their Coptic Christian heritage, along with the best education compared to the cities around us.

ED: Can you tell me how the school has grown in a short period of time?

Father Mina: We advertised a lot in the media, also on the Arabic channels, and in the churches around us. From this we got our kids. The people around us in the neighborhoods, when they see the school bus driving through the apartment complex, they ask and call, and that's where we get most of our kids—from the neighborhood communities around us, aside from the church.

ED: Has the Coptic community here in Troy and in Michigan grown over the last thirty years, or has it stayed steady?

Father Mina: We have flourished lately. Up until ten years ago we were only around two hundred families, and then all of a sudden the economy of Michigan was attracting people from other states and from Egypt. People were encouraging their relatives who were thinking about emigrating to come and settle here, and that's why in the last ten years we have seen a lot of growth. Probably we doubled our number.

ED: So across Michigan there are around 520 families in the church? How many people does that translate into, total?

Father Mina: If you multiply that by four or five it will give you roughly the number.

ED: What do you think people in Michigan need to know about the Copts? What would you like them to know?

Father Mina: We would love for them to get to know who we are, to visit our church.

ED: Can you describe the role of St. Mark Church in your community?

Father Mina: The youth groups are involved in helping the poor in Detroit. Our mission is to visit the families around us, and the nursing homes, and the hospitals. We participate in any charity or fundraising around us. We, as a church, also always respond to the gathering of the clergy in the city once a year. We participate in the clergy council, and that involves all activities in the Detroit area. We are a member of the Chamber of Commerce. We try to be active in any community effort that is around us.

ED: Is the church itself the hub or symbol of the Coptic community in Michigan?

Father Mina: That's where mainly Copts will gather, around the church. That was the situation back in Egypt; we gathered all our activities around the church. We would meet after the liturgy, after the Sunday school, after the praise of the evening, so always churches are the hubs of normal activities. The church here was built in 1979, but there were lots of additions to it later on. Pope Shenouda III laid the first brick, and also for this church, St. Mary. We call this area the St. Mark Cultural Center, which includes two churches: the Church of St. Mark and the Church of St. Mary, and also the Coptic school. The first time we prayed in this church [St. Mary] was last Christmas. Before we used to pray in the foyer, all of us would sit in the foyer. We entered only at Christmas.

ED: What are the biggest challenges that you and the Copts face in Michigan?

Father Mina: We have a challenge with the youth and what they see in the community and the diseases of the society, with their moral values . . . the drugs, the premarital sex. A lot of those things that will spoil the relation that we hope for our youth to have with the Lord. So we are struggling a lot nowadays with those kinds of diseases seeping in, because we as a church are part of society, and those things are coming into the church—the misuse of the Internet, the sex offenders, all those diseases are seeping in. So those are the challenges we face, because the mission of the church is preparing its members for eternity.

ED: Father Mina, many thanks!

An Interview with Father Maximus Habib

Grand Rapids, April 14, 2007

Eliot Dickinson (ED): Can you tell me your personal story and how you came to Michigan?

Father Maximus: I came in March of 1991 as a structural engineer, since I used to work for a construction company back home. We came in March, and I started studying for a Master's degree to find a job as an engineer, because the market is very slow. So I started at Wayne State and I took the Master's degree in 1995. I used to take just one class a semester, because I have a family—my wife Nancy and at the time one kid. She used to study to get her license as a medical doctor, she had to take exams and I had to support her also in studying and taking exams. In 1995 both of us started to work. She started her residency in Saginaw, and I started as an engineer in a very big firm, called Smith Group. I started there . . . as a fresh graduate, although I had ten years of experience and a Master's degree, and I took the first part of the Professional Engineer (PE) exam. I wanted to work in one of the big firms and was promoted twice in one year and in two years became a leader engineer. Thanks to God I did very well, and my wife worked as a doctor, and we were so happy and felt it was a great blessing.

Since we got married, something new happened every year. Father Mina asked me to help him out in the service. I used to serve as a deacon **59** and serve in Sunday school. I thought he was joking, and was leaving the next day to Florida for vacation. So I told him, "You know, Father Mina, I am busy, the kids are in the car and we are heading to Florida early in the morning." He asked me to think about it, and I was shocked, and it took me about six months to reach a decision. There is a common saying in our church that you cannot ask to be a priest, and you cannot refuse it. So after another six months, my wife and I reached the decision that I would serve.

ED: How did you leave Egypt and why did you settle in Michigan?

Father Maximus: When I got engaged to Nancy she told me that she is an American citizen. As soon as I heard this, I said, "Keep in mind, if you're planning to go to America, I don't want to leave my country." I was happy there, my church was everything to me, I had a good company and was starting to make money, and I was so happy. She said, "No, no [I don't want to leave]." This was 1989, and we got married in May 1990. By January 1991 I got sick of working back home, because it was so hard to make an honest living. So I started being unhappy. My wife was in her residency, but there was no opportunity to practice medicine, and she got sick of that system too. We thought about emigrating, and she said "Yes." This was in January, and in March I came and she came ten days after me (laughter). This was something we didn't plan at all, but this is how you feel God's hand moving and how it changed my heart.

ED: And how did you come to Michigan, in particular?

Father Maximus: I had a very old friend, he is the friend of my brother. We knew each other since I was seven years old, and I trusted him so much. Although I have family in New York and New Jersey, I trusted him and called him and asked if he would sponsor me. So when I came I spent about a month at his house, and then I moved and found a job.

ED: How many Copts are in Michigan, do you think?

Father Maximus: We have about 550 families.

ED: How do you define "Coptic," because there must be many dimensions of the identity. Do you have to be a member of the church, or from Egypt, or what?

Father Maximus: Yes, a member of the church.

ED: So if a Copt leaves the church, and says "I don't believe any more," then they are not Coptic any more?

Father Maximus: The confusion here comes from Copt as Egyptian and Copt as a religion. If he is not from the Coptic Orthodox [Church] he is not Coptic in the religious sense.

ED: So if I wanted to join the church, theoretically, could I become Coptic in the religious sense, but not the ethnic sense?

Father Maximus: Yes, because we have many Americans and Lebanese and others in our church.

ED: Would you ever accept an identity as an Arab? Do you ever consider yourself an Arab Christian?

Father Maximus: Never. Egyptian, 100 percent.

ED: Do you ever experience racism here in Michigan? That is, do people think you are Middle Eastern and not Christian?

Father Maximus: Yes, everywhere, this is why I use this leather cross. I have another cross in the car, which is bright silver, which is very clearly a cross. Many people think we are Muslims, because of how we look, our beards, our small hats. When I go to the airport, I don't even wear my hat, because most people don't know you can be Egyptian and Christian. I had the same story at both my jobs, they thought I was a Muslim for a long time, until I explained it.

ED: Did discrimination get worse after September 11, 2001?

Father Maximus: It's up and down, up and down.

ED: What challenges do you see for the Coptic community, or for yourself and your family, here in Michigan? Like racism, or discrimination, or keeping the faith alive, or growing the community, or anything like that.

Father Maximus: There are different challenges. For every Christian, to live Christ-like in a society which doesn't consider morals is a big challenge. To raise kids, especially, they see that everyone around them accepts things that are not right, which is a sin. I tell them, "you are American, but you are Christian." He or she cannot deny they are Christian. This is really a great challenge. Besides, even if you have lived here for thirty years, people still consider you a foreigner. But as soon as you are accepted, you are loved, you work hard at your job, using your God-given talent—then you get respect, and being a foreigner doesn't matter any more.

ED: And about the next generation, the children who come to the church, are you concerned that they will drift away from the church or from their heritage?

Father Maximus: This is a big challenge. Here in Michigan, about 80 percent of our youth are connected to the church. Some of them, the other 20 percent, they drift away after they settle and get married. It is a difficult challenge.

ED: Did you feel persecution in Egypt, for example Muslims against Christians? How would you characterize the situation for Copts in Egypt today?

Father Maximus: I'm not there on a daily basis, but from what I hear from my brothers and sisters and family, it's pretty bad. Although, if you live with someone for a long time and work with them for a long time, you find they are very good. For example, my brother owns a printing shop in Egypt and a girl who works there is a Muslim and she is wonderful. She is very honest, very polite, works very hard. This is an example. But from what I hear now, it's getting bad because of the fanaticism and Muslims who teach that Christians are idol worshipers and heretics.

ED: Are the Copts who are emigrating from Egypt now doing so because of persecution or economic reasons, or both?

Father Maximus: A combination, but mostly because of persecution.

ED: What denominations do you consider to be Coptic?

Father Maximus: Copts are Christians from Egypt, but if you are from any country and you join the Coptic Orthodox Church, you are going to be Coptic. It doesn't matter if you are American, or whoever, it doesn't matter. But again, there are some sister churches and we share the sacrament with them.

ED: As a researcher, what questions should I be asking about the Coptic community here in Michigan? What do you think I should I be looking for?

Father Maximus: You need to find out how Copts here practice their religion compared to back home in Egypt. Some people come here and tell us that our church is more spiritual and more strict than back in Egypt. We are trying to stay true to the core of our religion. However, we try to accommodate others, for example, like today, I used both Arabic and English in the liturgy.

ED: How do you keep in touch with Egypt? What are the ties that still connect you?

Father Maximus: I have brothers and sisters there, and I call regularly. I go back every four or five years, I'm going this June. The first time I went back I was so happy to see my family, my church where I grew up, the places, the monastery. I love that place, I love Cairo.

ED: Thank you so much!

Ethiopian Coptic Christians

embers of the Ethiopian Orthodox Tewahedo (or Unified) Church can legitimately be called Coptic Christians because of their historical and current link to the Coptic Orthodox Church. Christianity spread to Ethiopia in the fourth century A.D. when Frumentius, a Syrian Greek, was shipwrecked in present-day Eritrea while sailing through the Red Sea. Taken to the royal court, he was able to convert the Ethiopian Emperor Ezana to Christianity. Frumentius was eventually appointed bishop of Ethiopia by St. Athanasius, the patriarch of Alexandria. Today the Coptic Orthodox Church is considered the mother church of the Ethiopian Orthodox Tewahedo Church. The two churches are in communion, meaning that they recognize each other's baptisms and marriages, for example, and both are referred to as non-Chalcedonian Oriental Orthodox Churches.

The precise number of Ethiopian Christians in Michigan is unknown, but according to the priest at St. Mary Ethiopian Orthodox Tewahedo Church in Ferndale, a suburb of Detroit, about thirty or forty people regularly attend services, and as many as one hundred attend at Christmas and Easter. The services are held mostly in Amharic and Ge'ez, primarily because the church's priests and about one-quarter of the congregation are not sufficiently proficient in English. There is relatively little contact between St. Mary Ethiopian Church in Ferndale and St. Mark Coptic Church in Troy, as

St. Mary Ethiopian Orthodox Tewahedo Church in Ferndale, Michigan. Courtesy of Eliot Dickinson.

the two congregations stay in their own ethno-religious enclaves and rarely intermix.

Meskerem (Meskie) Gebreyohannes attends St. Mary Ethiopian Orthodox Tewahedo Church—that is, when she can escape for a few hours from her duties as proprietor of the *Taste of Ethiopia* restaurant at 29702 Southfield Road in Detroit. Originally from Ethiopia, she emigrated with her engineer-husband from Toronto, Canada, to Detroit, where she opened the eatery in 2005. The menu offers a mix of vegetarian and meat dishes that include red lentils, flatbread, lamb, beef, and chicken. Steaming hot towels are brought to wash the hands before the meal is served, because Ethiopian food is

Meskie Gebreyohannes.

traditionally eaten only with the fingers. One Detroit reviewer recounted her culinary experience this way:

> Even if you know and love the Ethiopian bread, *injera*, you may well not know that the scientific name of the grain, *Eragrostis tef,* comes from the Greek words *eros* (love) and *agrostis* (grass). At Taste of Ethiopia . . . the flavors cooked up by co-owner and chef Meskerem Gebreyohannes are so deep and so true, you may suspect you've never really experienced a lentil or a collard so intimately. You may start feeling a touch of *Eroslentilis* (Slaughter, "Out of Africa").

Meskie is not only co-owner, cook, and hostess, but also an adept conversationalist. She serves up delicious meals with a smile and chats up her customers in a friendly way, discussing all manner of subjects, including the goings-on in the local Ethiopian scene. A wide array of people frequent *Taste of Ethiopia,* but it is particularly popular among African immigrants and, on Wednesdays, members of the Ethiopian community in Detroit.

Coptic Recipes

Sitting with friends and socializing over a delicious meal is not only a sure way to enhance one's mood, but also to celebrate the joie de vivre. Breaking bread together is, indeed, a bonding experience and a way to experience a people's culture. It is also a serious matter for faithful Copts, who fast (i.e., abstain from milk, meat, fish, and eggs) for many days of the year, including fifty-five days before Easter and forty-five days before Christmas. Fortunately, there are many Arab food shops in Detroit and Dearborn, making it easy to find ingredients for favorite Egyptian meals throughout the year.

Let us remember the old saying by Jean Anthelme Brillat-Savarin "Tell me what you eat, and I will tell you who you are" when we consider what Pope Shenouda III opines about the virtues of vegetarianism: "Vegetal food is light, soft and soothing. It has nothing of the heaviness of meat and its grease and fat and whatever influence they have on one's body. We notice that even among animals the vicious and wild of them are carnivorous while the tame ones are herbivorous. Vegetarians are known to be quieter of nature than meat-eaters" (St. Mark, *Sharing Our Best*). With this in mind, the following vegetarian recipes present a petite sampling of Egyptian food, taken from a booklet entitled *Sharing Our Best: A Collection of Recipes by St. Mark Orthodox Church.*

Hummus Bil Tahini

1 1b. canned chickpeas, drained, save liquid
1–2 cloves garlic, crushed
3–5 Tbsp. tahini (sesame paste)
½ tsp. salt
¼–½ cup lemon juice
⅛ tsp. powdered cumin
2 Tbsp. olive oil

Place chickpeas (reserving 1 Tbsp. for garnish), garlic, tahini salt, lemon juice, and cumin in a blender, adding the saved liquid from the chickpeas to just below the level of the beans. Puree to a smooth, thick paste. If a thinner consistency is desired, add more liquid. Taste for seasoning and correct if necessary. Place in a shallow serving dish and cover with about 2 Tbsp. olive oil. Garnish by placing whole chickpeas in the center of the dish. Serve at room temperature with pita bread.

Hearty Lentil Soup

2½ cups dried lentils
12 cups water
1 cup onions, finely chopped
2 cups chopped celery
¼ cup oil
1 Tbsp. salt
1 8-oz. can tomato sauce
2 tsp. browning sauce
1 cup diced potatoes
2 cups thinly sliced carrots

Wash and drain lentils. Place in pot with 6 cups water. Bring to a boil. Lower heat and let simmer 45 minutes. Sauté onion and celery in oil in saucepan. Add cooked vegetables, 6 more cups of water, salt, tomato sauce, and browning sauce to lentils. Bring to boil. Add remaining ingredients. Cover and simmer about 30 minutes or until vegetables are tender. Serves ten.

Tamiyya (Falafel)

2 cups skinned white broad beans

½ cup fresh dill leaves

½ cup coriander leaves

2 onions

10 garlic cloves

½ cup parsley leaves

1 small leek, stalk only

1 Tbsp. cumin

½ Tbsp. cayenne pepper

1 Tbsp. baking soda

1–2 Tbsp sesame seeds

Cooking oil

Salt

Soak beans overnight. Drain and mince beans with the dill, coriander, onions, garlic, parsley, and leek. Add cumin, cayenne pepper, and baking soda and knead together. Let stand at room temperature 30 to 60 minutes. Scoop a small amount of mixture and shape into flat disks, about 2 inches in diameter. Sprinkle one side with sesame seeds and deep fry in hot oil until golden brown in color. Remove onto absorbent paper. Serve with bread, lettuce, tomato, and tahini.

Baklava

1 lb. pkg. of phyllo dough

½ cup Crisco

1 cup mixed nuts

½ cup sugar

1½ cup sugar

1 cup water

2 tsp. lemon juice

2 tsp. vanilla

Split the package of completely thawed phyllo dough into two layers (a bottom and a top layer). Put the bottom half in a greased 9 × 13-inch pan. Spread mixed nuts and ½ cup sugar on top. Then put the second layer of phyllo dough on top. With a knife, cut into small rectangles. Heat Crisco and spread it over the top. Bake in oven at 250 degrees for 1 hour and 10 minutes, or until baklava is light brown. While baklava is in oven, prepare syrup by mixing 1½ cup sugar, 1 cup water, 2 tsp. lemon juice, and 2 tsp. vanilla together in a saucepan over medium heat until sugar is dissolved. Remove baklava, and pour syrup on top.

Appendix 5

Coptic Ethnic Organizations

- **The American Coptic Association** offers all manner of news related to the Coptic Diaspora. For more information, contact the American Coptic Association, P.O. Box 55, Saddle River, N.J. 07458; *www.amcoptic.com*, and *amcoptic@usa.com*.

- **The American Coptic Union (ACU)** is a nonprofit organization originally established in 1992 in Jersey City, New Jersey, in response to the massacre of twelve Copts in Diarut in Upper Egypt. According to its Web site, the ACU speaks for both American and Egyptian Copts, in particular for women and children. It can be reached by fax at (201) 798–1451, and by e-mail at *freedom@copts4freedom.com*.

- **The Coptic Assembly of America (CAA)** is dedicated to promoting human rights and democracy in Egypt. It aims to work with American Copts and to lobby American politicians to improve the conditions of Copts in Egypt. Its stated goals are to build capacity in the Coptic diaspora, network with other human rights organizations, provide a voice for Coptic concerns, and meet with decision makers in Washington, D.C. The CAA can be visited online at *http://copticassembly.com*, and reached by mail at The Coptic Assembly of America, P.O. Box 452, Wilmette, Ill. 60091.

- **Coptic Orphans** seeks to help orphans and vulnerable children in Egypt. Its emphasis is on renewing hope and promoting children's education, health, and equality, including the empowerment of girls and young women. Those interested in helping can sponsor a child for $50 a month. For more information, contact Coptic Orphans: United States, P.O. Box 2881, Merrifield, Va. 22116; phone (703) 641-8910 or (800) 499-2989; fax (703) 641-8787; e-mail *info@copticorphans.org.*

The Copts United advances the interests of Copts in Egypt. Its Web site offers newspaper articles on the Copts, promotes Coptic art and culture, and posts the published proceedings of conferences held on the "Coptic Question." It can be reached at *www.coptsunited.com,* and *info@coptsunited.com.*

The Free Copts call for a secular Egypt and publish a magazine in English called *The Independent Copt,* available online at *http://freecopts.net/english.*

St. Mina Retreat Center, 743 W. Kneeland Road, Mio, Mich. 48647; phone (989) 826-6923; fax (989) 826-1204; e-mail *info@stminaretreatcenter.org;* Internet address *www.stminaretreatcenter.org.*

The University of Michigan Coptic Christian Student Association (CCSA) consists of about thirty students who meet twice weekly for dinner and prayer in Ann Arbor, Michigan. The CCSA can be contacted at 402 Hill St., Apt 1, Ann Arbor, Mich. 48104; phone (248) 227-1016; e-mail *mmegally@umich.edu.*

The U.S. Copts Association, founded in 1996, seeks to educate the global Coptic community on such issues as human rights, tolerance, and democracy. The group publishes the *Daily Coptic Digest,* an e-mail filled with calls for prayer, and hosts a Coptic discussion board on its Web site at *www.copts.com.* The U.S. Copts Association, 529 14th Street NW, Suite 1081, Washington, D.C. 20045; phone (202) 737-3660; fax: (202) 737-3661; e-mail *copts@copts.com.*

Notes

1. Father Mina is also often called "Abouna" or "Our Father" in Arabic.

2. Pope Shenouda III is quoted in the last sentence of *The Coptic Orthodox Church: A Lily Among Thorns* as saying "up till now there is no history book about the Coptic Orthodox Church in North America!" I hope here to have made my modest contribution. See Dr. Raafat Fahim Gindi, *The Coptic Orthodox Church: A Lily among Thorns* (Scarborough, Ontario: Mina Printing, n.d.), 190.

3. Hikaptah was the name of the ancient Egyptian city of Memphis, where Ptah was worshipped as a local deity. A less frequently noted (and less plausible) theory is that the word "Copt" is derived from the Upper Egypt city of Coptos, now called Quift. See Pierre du Bourguet, "Copt," in *The Coptic Encyclopedia*, edited by Aziz S. Atiya (New York: Macmillan, 1991).

4. *Aigyptios* is the adjective for Egyptian, whereas *Aigyptos* is the noun for Egypt.

5. Bourguet, "Copt."

6. Gindi, *The Coptic Orthodox Church*, 24-25. In full, the Church describes itself as Coptic (Egyptian), Orthodox (straight belief), One (one doctrine, belief, and entity), Sacred (in the body of Christ), Catholic (universal), and Apostolic (from the teaching of St. Mark the Apostle). I am grateful to Father Maximus Habib, who generously and without pause gave me a copy of this book, which is a sort of instructional guide for laypersons and Sunday school teachers alike.

7. *Webster's Encyclopedic Unabridged Dictionary of the English Language* (New York: Dilithium Press, 1989), s.v. "Copt."

8. Max Weber, "The Origins of Ethnic Groups," in *Ethnicity,* ed. John Hutchinson and Anthony D. Smith (Oxford: Oxford University Press, 1996), 35.

9. Friedrich Nietzsche, *Beyond Good and Evil* (Chicago: Henry Regnery Company, 1949), 165.

10. This church promotes African American pride and is led by Pastor Peter Banks, who calls himself "King Peter," wears what looks like a crown, and sits in a thronelike chair. The church asserts that African Americans are descendents of the ancient pharaohs as well as followers of the "Coptic Religion." See http://truetempleofsolomon.net.

11. John Davis is director of the Coptic Fellowship International, director of the Spiritual Unity of Nations (S.U.N.), as well as president of World Light Travels. At the Coptic Fellowship International annual conference in Olivet, Michigan, in June 2007, he spoke on the subject of "Preparing for the Quantum Leap." See http://www.coptic-sun.org.

12. John H. Watson, *Among the Copts* (Brighton: Sussex Academic Press, 2000), 84–85.

13. Bourguet, "Copt."

14. The author's friend, Adel Abadeer, is an Egyptian Copt from a Catholic family and a professor of economics at Calvin College in Grand Rapids, Michigan. He says that in Egypt he is referred to as a Catholic and not a Copt. However, in Michigan he identifies as a Copt and regularly attends the Coptic service in Grand Rapids. I would also like to thank my colleague, John Quinn, who teaches Coptic at Hope College, and points out that Coptic Catholics did accept the decisions made at the Council of Chalcedon, whereas members of the Coptic Church did not.

15. It should be noted that in everyday speech "Copt" can mean Christian, and in its original sense "Copt" also means Egyptian. The combinations "Coptic Christian" and "Egyptian Copt" may sound redundant, but are commonly used.

16. Anthony O'Mahoney, "Coptic Christianity in Modern Egypt," in *The Cambridge History of Christianity,* vol. 5, *Eastern Christianity,* ed. Michael Angold (Cambridge: Cambridge University Press, 2006), 493.

17. United States, *The World Factbook 1986* (Washington, D.C.:, U.S. Government Printing Office, 1986), 71; United States, *The World Factbook 1996* (Washington D.C.: Central Intelligence Agency, 1996), 141.

18. United States, *The World Factbook 2006* (Dulles, Va.: Potomac, 2006), 171. For the most current statistics, see also https://www.cia.gov/library/publications/the-world-factbook.

19. Raef Marcus, "Copts," in *Harvard Encyclopedia of American Ethnic Groups,* ed. Stephan Thernstrom (Cambridge: Harvard University Press, 1980).

20. Gabriel Abdelsayed, "Migration, Coptic," in *The Coptic Encyclopedia,* edited by Aziz S. Atiya (New York: Macmillan, 1991).

21. Marcus, "Copts"; Abdelsayed, "Migration, Coptic."

22. National Council of Churches, "Table 74: Religious Bodies—Selected Data," available online at http://www.ncccusa.org.

23. Mansour Sidhom, "Copts," in *Ethnic Groups in Michigan,* ed. James Anderson and Iva A. Smith (Detroit: Ethnos Press, 1983), 84–85.

24. U.S. Census Bureau, "The Arab Population: 2000," available online at http://www.census.gov/prod/2003pubs/c2kbr-23.pdf.

25. James Henry Breasted, *A History of Egypt: From the Earliest Times to the Persian Conquest,* 2d ed. (New York: Charles Scribner's Sons, 1912), 3.

26. Isa. 19:19; Matt 2:15, *Holy Bible: The New King James Version, Containing the Old and New Testaments* (Nashville: T. Nelson, 1982).

27. George Bullard, "Coptics Celebrate Millennium Anniversary of Christ's Flight to Egypt," *Detroit News,* 10 June 2000, C 6.

28. Meinardus notes that if Eusebius's *Ecclesiastical History* is correct, then St. Mark arrived between A.D. 41 and A.D. 44. See Otto F. A. Meinardus, *Two Thousand Years of Coptic Christianity* (Cairo: American University in Cairo Press, 1999), 64.

29. Dr. Raafat Fahim Gindi explains: "The term 'Monophysite,' started to be used from the 7th century by the Chalcedonian Churches to describe those who believe in the one nature of Christ. The right description of our [Coptic] Church is 'Miaphysite' which means one nature composite of two." Gindi, *The Coptic Orthodox Church,* 135.

30. For information on the statements of agreement between the Eastern Orthodox and Oriental Orthodox Churches regarding the debate over the "nature(s)" of Christ, see http://www.orthodoxunity.org/statements.html.

31. See, for example, Watson, *Among the Copts,* 145.

32. The precise moment when Copts became a minority is unclear, but some scholars say it occurred in the ninth century. See, for example, Jill Kamil, *Coptic Egypt: History and Guide* (Cairo: American University in Cairo Press, 1990), 41;

Meinardus, *Two Thousand Years of Coptic Christianity,* 64.

33. Muslim ideologues dispute the assertion that Copts were forced to convert to Islam. On this contested point, see Meinardus, *Two Thousand Years of Coptic Christianity,* 65; P. J. Vatikiotis, *The History of Egypt: From Muhammad Ali to Sadat* (Baltimore: Johns Hopkins University Press, 1980), 14. I am grateful to Dr. Ronald R. Stockton for bringing this matter to my attention.

34. In total, four languages are used in the Coptic liturgy in America: Arabic, Coptic, English, and Greek.

35. For a fascinating account of this time period, see Kyriakos Mikhail, *Copts and Moslems under British Control: A Collection of Facts and a Resume of Authoritative Opinions on the Coptic Question* (Port Washington, N.Y.: Kennikat Press, 1911). For background information on Egyptian history, see Tom Little, *Modern Egypt* (New York: Frederick A. Praeger, 1967); Vatikiotis, *The History of Egypt: From Muhammad Ali to Sadat;* and B. L. Carter, *The Copts in Egyptian Politics* (London: Croom Helm, 1986).

36. Edward Wakin, *A Lonely Minority: The Modern Story of Egypt's Copts* (New York: William Morrow and Company, 1963), 160.

37. Bourguet, "Copt."

38. Niloofar Haeri, *Sacred Language, Ordinary People: Dilemmas of Culture and Politics in Egypt* (New York: Palgrave Macmillan, 2003), 48.

39. Watson, *Among the Copts,* 148–9.

40. Kees Hulsman, "20 Coptic Christians Die as Village Tensions Flare," *Christianity Today,* 7 February 2000, 33.

41. Article 46 states: "The State shall guarantee the freedom of belief and the freedom of practicing religious rights." The Egyptian Constitution can be found on the internet at http://www.egypt.gov.eg/english/laws/constitution/index.asp.

42. Article 2 of the Egyptian Constitution states: "Islam is the Religion of the State. Arabic is its official language, and the principal source of legislation is Islamic Jurisprudence (Sharia)."

43. Recent reports indicate that unofficial "fatwas," or religious edicts that apply only to Muslims, have gotten out of hand in Egypt. See, for example, Michael Slackman and Mona El-Naggar, "A Compass That Can Clash with Modern Life," *New York Times,* 12 June 2007.

44. The INS was replaced by the Department of Homeland Security in 2002. Aristide Zolberg notes that the "fate of the INS, already in question before the [September 11, 2001] events, was sealed in early 2002 when the agency administered itself a

coup de grace by issuing student visa extensions to two of the hijackers six months after they died." Aristide Zolberg, *A Nation by Design: Immigration Policy in the Fashioning of America* (Cambridge: Harvard University Press, 2006), 447.

45. Marcus, "Copts."

46. Today Los Angeles has approximately thirty Coptic churches and its own Coptic bishop.

47. Marcus, "Copts."

48. Author's e-mail correspondence with Joanne Aneese, June 19, 2007.

49. Richard R. Jones, "Egyptian Copts in Detroit: Ethnic Community and Long-Distance Nationalism," in *Arab Detroit: From Margin to Mainstream,* ed. Nabeel Abraham and Andrew Shryock (Detroit: Wayne State University Press, 2000), 227.

50. Abdelsayed, "Migration, Coptic."

51. The precise length of Father Mikhail Melika's tenure in Troy is subject to debate. Richard R. Jones writes that he served from 1967 to 1977. However, Dr. Anis Milad believes he served for only a couple of years, perhaps from 1976 to 1977.

52. Delores Patterson, "Coptic Congregation Welcomes Patriarch—Pope Shenouda III's Troy Visit Is First to Area in 26 Years," *Detroit News,* 22 August 2003, D 1.

53. David Crumm, "Orthodox Families Awaiting Christmas," *Detroit Free Press,* 6 January 2007.

54. Author's e-mail correspondence with Joanne Aneese, June 19, 2007.

55. Music plays a significant role in the Coptic community. For example, the congregation's choir, or "Praising Group," has recorded a CD called *The Rock of Faith,* a collection of English and Arabic hymns. When Pope Shenouda visited Troy on August 22, 2007, a Coptic children's choir sang for him in front of approximately eight hundred people in St. Mary Church.

56. Author's e-mail correspondence with Joanne Aneese, June 19, 2007.

57. Ibid. Sports play an important role in the lives of Coptic youths, just as they do for many young Americans. However, while there is an Orthodox Basketball League, most young Michigan Copts participate in organized sports at their schools or recreationally on their own.

58. Sidhom, "Copts," 85.

59. Father Mina Essak of St. Mark Church, interview by author, 20 April 2007, Troy, Michigan.

60. Ibid.

61. Father Maximus Habib of St. Mark Church, interview by author, 14 April 2007,

Grand Rapids, Michigan.

62. Richard R. Jones, "Egyptian Copts in Detroit," 235.

63. My thanks to John W. Smith, who literally pointed out to me the hyperplural-
ism of Detroit's northside suburbs. As we drove through the back streets doing
fieldwork, checking out the rich kaleidoscope of Orthodox Churches and discussing Michigan's ethno-religious complexity, we were happy researchers in
our element.

64. For a thorough listing of Coptic names, see Appendix A in Meinardus, *Two
Thousand Years of Coptic Christianity.*

65. The U.S. Copts Association is located in Washington, D.C. Its Web site contains
information about the Copts, daily news pertaining to the global Coptic community, and a Coptic discussion board in English and Arabic. Interested can-
didates can even apply to intern at the association—applications are reviewed
on a rolling basis. The Association describes itself as a "nonprofit organization
dedicated to raising awareness of human rights abuses against Copts within
Egypt and educating the Coptic community both in Egypt and throughout the
international diaspora on human rights advocacy, democratic development,
and religious freedom." See http://www.copts.com/english.

66. Gregory Katz, "The Silent Exodus: Extremist Landscape in Egypt Is Where Violence Takes Hold," *Houston Chronicle,* 26 December 2006, A 1.

67. Youssef Sidhom, "Problems on Hold: Shame on Reconciliation!" *Watani Newspaper,* (accessed 29 May 2007). The *Watani Newspaper* Web site (http://wataninet.
com) states: "*Watani* is an Egyptian weekly Sunday newspaper published in Cairo.
The word Watani is Arabic for 'My Homeland.' The paper was founded in 1958 by
the prominent Copt Antoun Sidhom (1915–1995), who strove for the establishment
of a civil, democratic society in Egypt, where all Egyptians would enjoy full citizen-
ship rights regardless of their religious denomination. This remains *Watani*'s ob-
jective to this day, leaning neither left nor right on the political level, but following
its own clear course in the press field. Those in charge of *Watani* view this role as
a patriotic all-Egyptian vocation, especially following the increasing marginalisa-
tion of the Coptic role, issues and culture within the Egyptian society over the past
half century. *Watani* is deeply dedicated to offer its readers high quality, extensive,
credible press coverage, with special focus on Coptic issues, culture, heritage, and
contribution to Egyptian society" (accessed 7 July 2007).

68. See, for example, the SAT-7 Satellite Television Service (www.sat7.org/). To
join an electronic forum for Coptic Orthodox Christians and receive the "Daily

Digest of the Coptic Network" e-mail, contact: copt-net@cs.bu.edu. Be prepared to receive regular e-mails with a long prayer list, but limited information. A free "Coptic" e-mail account can also be acquired by signing up at: http://www .copticmail.com.

69. Matt. 5:10, *Holy Bible.*

70. Father Maximus Habib of St. Mark Church, interview by author, April 14, 2007, Grand Rapids, Michigan.

71. Wakin, *A Lonely Minority,* 134.

72. Jones, "Egyptian Copts in Detroit," 230.

73. Tulips are common in Western Michigan, where many Dutch immigrants settled.

74. Also fascinating is the chorus of praise to "Ilah" (not to be confused with "Allah"). "Ilah" is a generic term for God in Arabic, and in the Coptic liturgy it refers to the Persons of the Trinity.

75. Meinardus, *Two Thousand Years of Coptic Christianity,* 3.

76. O'Mahoney, "Coptic Christianity in Modern Egypt," 508.

77. Abdelsayed, "Migration, Coptic."

78. One of the nineteen hijackers on September 11, 2001, was a Muslim Egyptian.

79. Andrea Elliot, "A Bloody Crime in New Jersey Divides Egyptians Once Again," *New York Times,* 21 January 2005.

80. The 2003 Detroit Arab American Study (DAAS) provides a wealth of information on Detroit's Arab and Chaldean communities, but has very little on the Copts. See the "Preliminary Findings from the Detroit Arab American Study," by Wayne Baker et al., available online at http://www.umich.edu/news/Releases/2004/ Jul04/daas.pdf (accessed 18 December 2007).

81. Jones, "Egyptian Copts in Detroit," 234.

82. However, polls indicate that while some 85 percent of Americans self-identify as Christian, half cannot name even one of the four Gospels. For an insightful article on this subject, see Bill McKibben, "The Christian Paradox: How a Faithful Nation Gets Jesus Wrong," *Harper's Magazine,* August 2005.

83. Meinardus, *Two Thousand Years of Coptic Christianity,* 265.

84. George W. Bush once referred to a "crusade" against terrorism. Alongside self-righteous posturing and the destruction of Iraq—the location of the biblical Garden of Eden—this looks very much like a sad repetition of history.

85. See Jones, "Egyptian Copts in Detroit," 219.

For Further Reference

Books and Articles

Abdelsayed, Gabriel. "Migration, Coptic." In *The Coptic Encyclopedia,* edited by Aziz S. Atiya. New York: Macmillan, 1991.

Badr, Habīb, Souad Abou el-Rousse Slim, and Jūzīf Abū Nahrā, eds. *Christianity: A History in the Middle East.* Beirut, Lebanon: Middle East Council of Churches, Studies & Research Program, 2005.

Bourguet, Pierre du. "Copt." In *The Coptic Encyclopedia,* edited by Aziz S. Atiya. New York: Macmillan, 1991.

Boutros-Ghali, Boutros. *An Agenda for Peace.* New York : United Nations, 1995.

———. *Egypt's Road to Jerusalem: A Diplomat's Story of the Struggle for Peace in the Middle East.* New York: Random House, 1997.

———. *Unvanquished: A U.S.-U.N. Saga.* New York: Random House, 1999.

Breasted, James Henry. *A History of Egypt: From the Earliest Times to the Persian Conquest.* 2d ed. New York: Charles Scribner's Sons, 1912.

Bullard, George. "Coptics Celebrate Millennium Anniversary of Christ's Flight to Egypt." *Detroit News,* 10 June 2000, C 6.

Carter, B. L. *The Copts in Egyptian Politics.* London: Croom Helm, 1986.

Crumm, David. "Orthodox Families Awaiting Christmas." *Detroit Free Press,* 6 January 2007.

Divine Liturgies of Saints Basil, Gregory and Cyril. S.I: Printed by Verena Design, 2001.

Elliot, Andrea. "A Bloody Crime in New Jersey Divides Egyptians Once Again." *New York Times,* 21 January 2005.

Gindi, Dr. Raafat Fahim. *The Coptic Orthodox Church: A Lily Among Thorns.* Scarborough, Ontario: Mina Printing, n.d.

Griggs, C. Wilfred. *Early Egyptian Christianity: From its Origins to 451 C.E.* Leiden: E. J. Brill, 1990.

Haeri, Niloofar. *Sacred Language, Ordinary People: Dilemmas of Culture and Politics in Egypt.* New York: Palgrave Macmillan, 2003.

Holy Bible: The New King James Version, Containing the Old and New Testaments. Nashville: T. Nelson, 1982.

Hulsman, Kees. "20 Coptic Christians Die as Village Tensions Flare." *Christianity Today,* 7 February 2000, 31-33.

Jones, Richard R. "Egyptian Copts in Detroit: Ethnic Community and Long-Distance Nationalism." In *Arab Detroit: From Margin to Mainstream,* edited by Nabeel Abraham and Andrew Shryock, 219-40. Detroit: Wayne State University Press, 2000.

Kamil, Jill. *Coptic Egypt: History and Guide.* Cairo: American University in Cairo Press, 1990.

Katz, Gregory. "The Silent Exodus: Extremist Landscape in Egypt is Where Violence Takes Hold." *Houston Chronicle,* 26 December 2006, A 1.

Little, Tom. *Modern Egypt.* New York: Frederick A. Praeger, 1967.

Marcus, Raef. "Copts." In *Harvard Encyclopedia of American Ethnic Groups,* edited by Stephan Thernstrom. Cambridge: Harvard University Press, 1980.

McKibben, Bill. "The Christian Paradox: How a Faithful Nation Gets Jesus Wrong." *Harper's Magazine,* August 2005, 31-37.

Meinardus, Otto F. A. *Two Thousand Years of Coptic Christianity.* Cairo: American University in Cairo Press, 1999.

Mikhail, Kyriakos. *Copts and Moslems under British Control: A Collection of Facts and a Resume of Authoritative Opinions on the Coptic Question.* Port Washington, N.Y.: Kennikat Press, 1911.

Nietzsche, Friedrich. *Beyond Good and Evil.* Chicago: Henry Regnery Company, 1949.

O'Mahony, Anthony. "Coptic Christianity in Modern Egypt." In *The Cambridge History of Christianity.* Vol. 5, *Eastern Christianity,* edited by Michael Angold, 488-510. Cambridge: Cambridge University Press, 2006.

Patterson, Delores. "Coptic Congregation Welcomes Patriarch—Pope Shenouda III's Troy Visit Is First to Area in 26 Years." *Detroit News,* 22 August 2003, D 1.

Peace News (Majallat al-sala¯m). Detroit, Mich.: s.n, 1978.

Sidhom, Mansour. "Copts." In *Ethnic Groups in Michigan,* edited by James Anderson and Iva A. Smith. Detroit: Ethnos Press, 1983.

Slackman, Michael, and Mona El-Naggar. "A Compass That Can Clash with Modern Life." *New York Times,* 12 June 2007.

Slaughter, Jane. "Out of Africa." *Metro Times: Detroit's Weekly Alternative,* 7 December 2005.

St. Mark Coptic Orthodox Church. *Sharing Our Best: A Collection of Recipes.* Kearney, Neb.: Morris Press, 2001.

United States. *The World Factbook 1986.* Washington, D.C.: U.S. Government Printing Office, 1986.

United States. *The World Factbook 1996.* Washington, D.C.: Central Intelligence Agency, 1996.

United States. *The World Factbook 2006.* Dulles, Va.: Potomac, 2006.

Vatikiotis, P. J. *The History of Egypt: From Muhammad Ali to Sadat.* 2d ed. Baltimore: Johns Hopkins University Press, 1980.

Wakin, Edward. *A Lonely Minority: The Modern Story of Egypt's Copts.* New York: William Morrow and Company, 1963.

Watson, John H. *Among the Copts.* Brighton: Sussex Academic Press, 2000.

Weber, Max. "The Origins of Ethnic Groups." In *Ethnicity,* edited by John Hutchinson and Anthony D. Smith, 35–39. Oxford: Oxford University Press, 1996.

Webster's Encyclopedic Unabridged Dictionary of the English Language. New York: Dilithium Press, 1989.

Wiens, Claudia Yvonne. *Coptic Life in Egypt.* Cairo: American University in Cairo Press, 2003.

Zolberg, Aristide. *A Nation by Design: Immigration Policy in the Fashioning of America.* Cambridge: Harvard University Press, 2006.

Web Sites

Http://www.coptic.net (has a link to Alexandria Coptic Radio, which broadcasts live Coptic music, prayers, and Pope Shenouda III's sermons in Arabic).

Http://www.copticchurch.net (provides daily readings and commemorations, many links, and the locations of all Coptic churches in the United States).

Http://www.copts.com (offers English and Arabic news articles on the Copts, as well as an archive dating back to 1997).

Http://st-takla.org (contains an image gallery, a kid's corner, an online dictionary, online hymns, lectures, videos, books, and more).

Http://www.amcoptic.com (offers an assortment of English and Arabic articles related to the Coptic diaspora).

Http://www.suscopts.org (is the site of the Coptic Orthodox Diocese of the Southern United States, which represents Coptic communities in Alabama, Arizona, Arkansas, Florida, Georgia, Louisiana, Mississippi, New Mexico, Oklahoma, Tennessee, and Texas).

Http://www.copticorthodox.com (provides numerous links to sites selling church-related gifts, magazines, and apparel).

Http://www.orthodoxunity.org (is the site of Orthodox Unity, an organization dedicated to facilitating dialogue between the Eastern and Oriental Orthodox Churches).

Http://copticassembly.com (offers a rich source of political information, editorials, and Coptic news).

Http://www.coptsunited.com (supplies an array of articles, press releases, and Coptic political declarations).

Http://freecopts.net (contains an archive of the *The Independent Copt* magazine).

Index

B

Banks, Pastor Peter, 76 (n. 10)

Bemha, 39

Benedict XVI, Pope, 15

Bethlehem, 12

Big Rapids, 42

Bloomfield Hills, 9

Bonaparte, Napoleon, 18

Boston, 8

Boulos, Roushdy, 24, 25

Bourguet, Pierre du, 3, 6

Boutros-Ghali, Boutros, 21, 22, 37

Bowling Green State University, 36

Brain drain, 33, 50

Breasted, James Henry, 11

Brillat-Savarin, Jean Anthelme, 69

Bush, George W., 81 (n. 84)

Byzantine Eastern Roman Empire, 16

C

Cairo, 15, 20, 21, 29, 39, 63, 80 (n. 67)

Cairo University, 15, 21

Calvin College, 76 (n. 14)

Canada, 21, 25, 36, 54, 66

Chalcedonian Churches, 14, 77 (n. 29)

Chicago, 8, 25, 51, 52

Christianity, 11, 37, 43, 46, 47, 53

Christmas, 22, 28, 30, 37, 57, 65, 69

Cleveland, 8

Columbia University, 21

Copt: definition of, 3, 4, 53, 54; etymol-
ogy of, 3

Coptic Assembly of America, 73

Coptic Church Review, 38

Coptic Fellowship International, 5, 6,
76 (n. 11)

Coptic language, 12, 15, 16, 28, 43, 48, 55,
56; dialects of, 14; script, 11, 12, 14, 18

Coptic Orphans, 73

Coptic people: Catholics, 6, 76 (n. 14);
Christians, 6, 14, 20, 36, 38, 65;
diaspora of, 15, 18, 19, 38, 39, 43, 44,
73, 80 (n. 65), 86; emigration of,
19, 22, 29, 37, 49; identity of, 45–48;
immigration of, 21, 23; names of,
36–37, 80 (n. 64); population of, 7,
46; recipes of, 69–72

Coptic religious institutions: Catholic
Church, 4; Orthodox Church, 4, 6,
7, 8, 13, 14, 16, 24, 35, 36, 40, 42, 53,
62, 65; revival of, 15, 43–44

Coptic symbols: cross, 26, 42, 46, 47, 54,
61; icon(s), 1, 13, 41

Coptic Theological Seminary, 15

Coptos, 75 (n. 3)

Copts United, 74

Council of Chalcedon, 14, 16, 76 (n. 14)

Cyprus, 13

Cyril VI, Pope, 15, 25

Cyrus, 16

D

Daily Coptic Digest, 74

Dar al-Qubt, 3

Davis, John, 76 (n. 11)

Demotic, 12

Desert Fathers, 31

Detroit Arab American Study (DAAS),
81 (n. 80)

Detroit auto industry 24, 34, 52

Diarut, 73

Divine Liturgies of Saints Basil, Gregory,